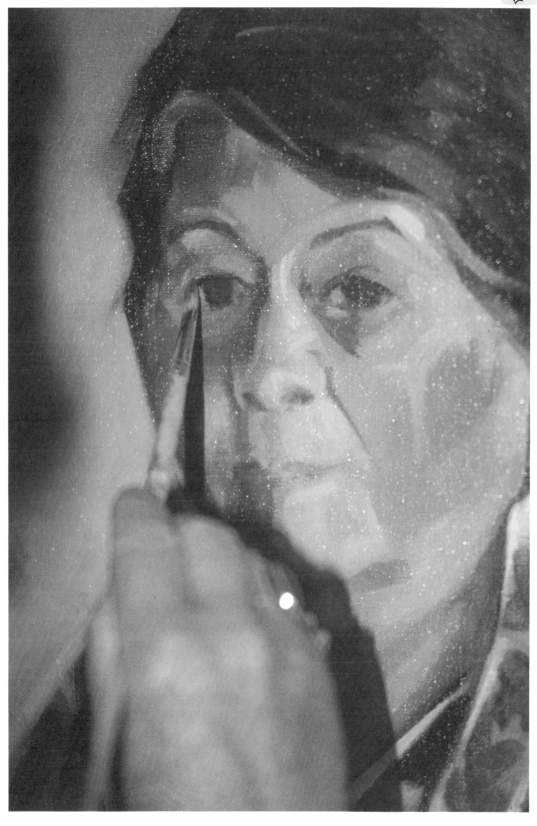

Chronicles of Pride

A Journey of Discovery

by Patricia Richardson Logie

Detselig Enterprises Limited
Calgary, Alberta

Canadian Cataloguing in Publication Data
 Richardson, Patricia Logie.
        Chronicles of pride

    ISBN 1-55059-012-X

    1. Indians of North America - Canada - Biography.
2. Indians of North America - Canada - Portraits.
3. Métis - Biography.*   4. Métis - Portraits.*
5. Inuit - Canada - Biography.*   6. Inuit - Canada
- Portraits.*   I. Title.
E89.R52 1990   971'.00497'0922   C90-091283-9

Detselig Enterprises Limited
P.O. Box G 399
Calgary, Alberta T3A 2G3

Printed in Canada   SAN 115-0324   ISBN 1-55059-012-X

A series of thirty-one oil paintings of contemporary Canadian Aboriginal people who are contributing to the Indian community as well as the community at large.

From the first stroke of the brush to the last moment,

when I breathe life into the painting, it is a constant celebration of positive life forces.

NOTE

This book uses several different terms to refer generically to the indigenous or aboriginal people of Canada. It uses the terms "Indian", "First Nations", and "Native", "Aboriginal" and "Indigenous" people interchangeably with the understanding that these terms convey the respect intended. There is apparently little agreement among the people concerned as to the best term; by using various alternatives in this document, it is hoped that no one will be offended.

Detselig Enterprises Ltd. appreciates the financial assistance for its 1990 publishing program from

Canada Council
Alberta Foundation for the Literary Arts

Dedication

When I look back into my childhood, the circumstances of my life seem like stepping stones along a path, each stone leading me closer to my goal. Which consciously came first, the goal or the means to the goal, or which really was the goal, the means or the end, I do not know. All I do know is that the whole floated within me, not having substance or direction until the stones suddenly came to a halt before a door. While I constantly searched with open mind and heart, the key magically materialized and slowly, I opened the door.

What circumstances or what voice within a child could move the footstep toward the first stone along that specific path?

Beyond the door there were many kind hearts and smiling faces smoothing my path and I knew with certainty that they had been waiting.

The need for me to express my feelings about Indian people, I have discovered, goes back to my youth; back to a man I loved and respected who had a profound influence on me—my father—who believed as Gandhi did, that all men are brothers. So essentially, this project was initiated by my father many years ago.

And so for Dickie and his abiding love.

Contents

Preface 1

About the Artist by Tam W. Deachman 2

Foreword by Georges Erasmus 3

Introduction 5

The Catalyst for Chronicles Of Pride   7

Daphne Odjig 10

Lyle Wilson 16

Yvonne Dunlop 22

A Journey Of Discovery   27

Margo Kane 30

Dorothy Francis 36

Dr. Louis Miranda 42

Marjorie Cantryn White 46

John Williams 52

Glen Newman 60

George Manuel 66

Gloria George 72

Simon Baker 78

Vivian Wilson 84

Leonard George 88

Verna Kirkness 94

Paul Willie 100

Blanche Macdonald .106

Peggy Shannon 112

Matthew Hill 116

Judge Alfred Scow 122

Guujaaw 128

David Gladstone 134

Pauline Waterfall 140

Walter Harris 146

Senator Len Marchand 152

Chief Joe Mathias, Bill Wilson, Chief James Gosnell 158

Brenda Taylor 164

Mildred Gottfriedson .170

Robert Sterling 176

Agnes Alfred 182

A Promise 188

Conclusion 193

Acknowledgments 196

Some art instructors and various schools of art, through lack of knowledge, will comment that portraiture is not an art form. But, composition, surface tension, negative and positive space, color and concept are all part of good portraiture. And in portraiture, one must go further and look beyond form and three dimensions. One must learn to read the inner person, the spirit, through a one-to-one relationship. One doesn't remember the color of the eye or the shape of the eyebrow, but does remember how it feels to be with a person and that is what has to be painted.

Portraiture is one of the most difficult areas of painting; it chooses you, you do not choose portraiture. It steals into your being and you must abide. Then it must be, that the artist who is chosen to work in this field has an inordinate affinity for humankind.

As a teacher of portraiture, this is what I try to instill in my students, but it comes in small bits and pieces and takes a very long time to grow. It was a natural progression that engulfed me in this difficult and broadly-scoped project and I am still learning how to show the respect I feel for the people I write about. I know it shows in the paintings.

PATRICIA RICHARDSON LOGIE

About the Artist

"I don't like to paint from photographs," says Patricia Logie, "because that would simply be copying what the camera has seen, and I have no idea whether the camera has caught the real person. I want each portrait to have a unique something about it; the pose, the tilt of the head, the positioning of the hands, even the direction of the gaze, which will say something very basic, very essential, about how I feel the person relates to their world."

This uncanny ability of Patricia Richardson Logie to put personality on canvas began to emerge at a very early age. Born in Niagara Falls, Ontario, she found she had an irresistible urge to sketch her classmates when she should have been studying. By the time she was 16, her talent had come to the attention of pastel painter Tom Layton. Two years later she began to work with oils.

She married Robert Logie at 21, but continued painting as she busied herself raising a family during the 50s and 60s. In 1970, they took two of their four children to England for a year. Here Patricia enrolled in Sir John Cass College, then a combined arts and crafts school. She exhibited in a two-woman show in London, and had work accepted for the Royal Society of Portrait Painters' Exhibition which toured major galleries in England, and also by the Pastel Society.

On her return to British Columbia in 1971, and still with very little in the way of formal art education, she began to devote more and more time to painting. She entered shows and continued to send work to England. By 1977, her work so impressed London's Society of Women Artists, that they asked her to stand for membership. Her membership was granted in 1979, the same year in which she became an Associate of the Federation of Canadian Artists.

She was commissioned by the Mendel Gallery, Saskatoon, to paint F.S. Mendel for the Permanent Collection. She has had one-woman shows in the Mendel Gallery, the Burnaby Gallery, the Gainsborough Gallery, Calgary, and the Palette Gallery, Vancouver. Other exhibitions in Vancouver include Galerie Royale, Raymond Chow Gallery, Harrison Gallery and Griffin's Gallery West. Her paintings are included in the Vancouver School Board Collections and in many private collections in the United States, Japan, England and across Canada.

TAM W. DEACHMAN
1980

Throughout history, prominent Indian leaders such as Crowfoot, Chief of the Blackfeet, Tecumseh, mystic Chief of the Shawnee, Louis Riel, leader of the Bois Brulés and Poundmaker, Chief of the Cree have been recognized by all.

The contribution by Indian leaders to the development of the Western world took on many forms, most of which found our ancestors either in a protecting role or forced to aggressive outbursts over the struggle for the land.

Today those struggles continue. The tactics are more civilized and the faces are different, but the issues remain consistent. People of the First Nations are strong in their beliefs, adamant in their struggle and draw power from their knowledge. Their self-esteem is strongly intact.

Within the Native community in Canada, we witness the strides and accomplishments of individuals who work endlessly toward fulfilling the goals of intimacy with one's environment. To further cultivate the idea, domestically and internationally, we must develop avenues of communications together. We must learn to understand and accept one another and appreciate each other's individuality, goals and achievements. Each person deserves the respect of another.

From the younger generations, who must learn from the wisdom of the older generation, the cycle of life will prevail. The values and intent of living in harmony with one's self and one's environment must be instilled in the young. This example starts with the birth of a human being and the fostering of his or her growth to appreciate and accept that which cannot be changed and to provide the courage to change that which must be changed.

The individuals portrayed in the following pages are an example of that leadership, contributing in their own way to make a better life—to procure harmony and unity in all living things.

GEORGES ERASMUS
National Chief
Assembly of First Nations

Introduction

The discovery in 1982 that I had to paint this series for my own growth and for the little I could contribute, satisfied a long, deep-rooted desire; one from which I had so often turned away. But sometimes there is a moment when all roads meet in your mind and if in that moment you listen, you will learn which road you must take. The road led me through one moving experience to another and I was grateful to be involved.

The spirituality of the people I painted struck a resounding chord in me and I was able to paint with love and feeling. An artist cannot always expect to receive the vibrations needed from the sitter to paint an outstanding picture, but the inspirational level was high.

Daphne Odjig, Yvonne Dunlop and Lyle Wilson were the beginning. In 1979, I met Daphne Odjig through a mutual friend. I was impressed by her concepts, her physical presence and good looks. A portrait of Daphne Odjig and her work would also be impressive. Lyle Wilson and Yvonne Dunlop were Native Indian Teacher Education Program (NITEP) students at the University of British Columbia, and as all students need to earn funds for school, I hired them as models. These students were wonderful to paint. Their high cheekbones and strong features were of great interest to me as a painter, and their personalities, inner strength and determination added more color to the paintings.

In my new awareness, I realized that all the illustrations of First Peoples were of warriors or underprivileged, woebegone figures of a dying race. Where were the Native people I knew? Nowhere in my search could I find the people of this generation who are working and striving to help the image of their people through involvement in education, in the artistic community, in politics, in business, in law, and in the general struggle to keep the Indian culture alive and of consequence. I had no choice—as an artist I had to portray these people so that everyone might become aware of their contributions. This was the introduction to a life's work.

Chronicles of Pride became a series of 31 paintings dealing with the concept of both awareness and role modeling; of personal pride and human dignity; of the rewards of open communication and knowledge of other cultures. I found my subjects by searching and listening, and by communicating. The original decision to immortalize these people on canvas has developed into a broad project that has taken on a life of its own.

Pacific Western and BC Air graciously flew me to reserves outside of Vancouver to allow me to paint some of the subjects. Canadian Airlines flew the completed exhibition to nine destinations throughout British Columbia, and flew me in to speak to adults and children about the accomplishments of the people painted. The eyes of many were opened, and in others a feeling of pride and/or humility were born. A list of goals was made early on in the project and those goals are slowly being reached:

- an exhibition to tour through British Columbia, Canada, the United States, Germany and Japan;

- an educational program for schools and the public;

- a book, including colored reproductions of the painting and the story of the journey;

- a postage stamp commemorating the aboriginals indigenous to Canada through *Chronicles of Pride*;

- a permanent home for the exhibit so it will be remembered that:

  - anyone can accomplish and make a contribution,

  - each of us is special whatever our heritage,

  - we must learn to be proud of ourselves.

The Catalyst for
Chronicles of Pride

. . . she was preparing for her Vancouver show,
"Time Passages".

Painting #1
size: 30 x 42 (76.2 cm x 106.68 cm)

Daphne Odjig Beavon (1919 -)

Artist

Daphne Odjig was born at Wikwemikong Reserve, Manitoulin Island, Ontario, on September 11, 1919. She is of the Odawa tribe, Ojibway Nation.

In her long career as an artist, Daphne "ODJIG" transcended many traditional barriers for Native people in the arts and became an internationally known painter. One of her best known works is the eight-foot by twenty-seven foot (244 cm x 823 cm) mural entitled "The Indian in Transition" (1978). It was commissioned by the National Museum of Man and is exhibited in the National Arts Centre in Ottawa. Daphne also illustrated *Tales From the Smokehouse*, a collection of Native stories. She received an Honorary Doctorate (LLD) from the University of Toronto for her work in the field of art and she received the Order of Canada for her artistic contribution to her country.

I wanted to show Daphne as the colorful, strong, but unassuming person she is, with paintings from her series *Time Passages* in the background.

Daphne Odjig

With the consent of Daphne Odjig, I travelled by plane to Anglemont, British Columbia on Shuswap Lake, with my giraffe-legged easel, my paints and a large canvas in tow. The plane was met by Daphne, the subject of my first painting.

Daphne's and her husband Chester's home was a warm, friendly place, and I was made to feel welcome. I was included in the life of the house and the surrounding neighborhood. Chester helps Daphne in all things and is a constant support. They live in a quiet wooded spot that slopes down to a beautiful lake, and from her studio Daphne sees the ever-changing moods of water and sky that inspire her.

I saw the building in which Daphne had painted her large (27' x 8') mural *Indian in Transition*, and I was interested in how she had managed that size of canvas. She had rented an empty house with large spaces and her husband had built a special stretcher. The canvas hung suspended and braced. I painted her in her studio where she was preparing for her Vancouver show *Time Passages* held in October 1979. The patterns that surround Daphne in the painting are impressions of her canvases for that show.

Through Daphne, I first became aware of Indian art and mythology. I discovered that much Native work was symbolic of the many animals found in the myths and traditions of the culture. Legends and stories about such animals as the bear, the raven, the eagle, the frog, the beaver, the whale, the wolf, salmon and many more are illustrated in paintings, drawings and in carvings for masks, boxes, bowls and totem poles. These legends tell of the beginning of time and other important events that formed the culture. While with Daphne, I took the first stepping stone in a learning experience which I hope will continue throughout my life.

Daphne has become well known throughout Canada. Her symbolic figures and the simple signature "ODJIG" appear in many prestigious places including the Manitoba Museum of Man and Nature; the National Museum of Man in Ottawa (recently renamed the Museum of Civilization); the collection of the government of Israel, Jerusalem, in the "Jerusalem Series" commissioned by El Al Airlines; and the McMichael Canada Collection in Kleinberg, Ontario, to name a few. She received an Honorary Doctorate of Letters from Laurentian University in 1982; a Doctorate of Letters, from the University of Toronto in

1985; was Elected R.C.A. in 1989; and her country has given her the Order of Canada. As well, she treasures an eagle feather presented to her by Chief Wakageshig from the people of Wikwemiking.

She was born in 1919 at the Wikwemiking Reserve in Ontario and is an Ojibway Indian of the Odawa Nation, daughter of Dominic. She is tall and slim, a handsome woman, quiet spoken and unassuming. She wears large silver and turquoise jewellery crafted by her American counterparts. She presented an interesting subject for a painting, and when the impression of her own paintings was introduced onto the canvas it became a strong composition.

Daphne has struggled, as all artists do, to have her work known and appreciated. In her early days she painted traditionally, but in the long search, she finally came to rest with her symbolic, mythological, colorful paintings. In 1985, she had a retrospective exhibition at the Thunder Bay National Exhibition Centre. When artists have a retrospective, they finally become aware of the route they have taken and where it has led them.

Daphne and I worked well together. So often when artists are being painted, they cannot contain themselves and insist on introducing their concepts of how the painting should look or what the artist should say about the subject. With good grace, Daphne did not follow the norm; she sat attentively and patiently until the canvas was completed.

After a day or two of drying, the painting was carefully crated, my easel once more collapsed and we were on our way flying back to Vancouver, the painting of Daphne, and me. The painting showed the strength and dignity of this woman and her quiet pride. I was pleased with what had come out on the canvas and what had seeped into my mind.

*. . . so I used the dark muted tones and emphasized
his powerful hand and forearm.*

Painting #2
Size: 24 x 30 (60.96 cm x 76.2 cm)

Lyle Wilson (1955 -)

Artist

Lyle Wilson comes from Kitimat, British Columbia. He was born at Butedale Cannery and is a member of the Haisla-Kwagiutl language group.

Lyle Wilson is a carver of silver and wood, who uses contemporary concepts within a Northwest Coast style. He works on many creative projects for the University of British Columbia's Museum of Anthropology. Lyle Wilson attended the Native Indian Teacher Education Program (NITEP) and then majored in art while doing his teaching degree at the University of British Columbia. He also attended the Emily Carr School of Art, studying lithography, etching and graphics.

I was introduced to Lyle as a model for some of my paintings when he was attending the Native Indian Teacher Education Program. In painting him, I wanted to present the quiet strength of this young man. Therefore, I used dark, muted tones and emphasized his powerful hand and forearm. In his hand he clasps a silver bracelet which he has carved.

Lyle Wilson

After my happy experience with Daphne, I was even more interested in doing the thing I said I would never do—paint Native Indians. I had the feeling that these people had been used by artists to paint pretty little pictures.

At a social gathering I spoke to Bev Berger, who was at that time coordinator of the Native Indian Teacher Education Program, and she suggested that I should hire the students as models. Bev invited me to a barbecue to be held at the NITEP huts on the university campus to meet the students. I saw many who would fill the bill as models, but finally it was Yvonne Dunlop and Lyle Wilson who were chosen.

I met Lyle Wilson in the silkscreen room at the Emily Carr College of Art in Vancouver. He promised he would come to the studio to be painted. When he appeared at my studio door he was quiet, reserved and serious. I immediately felt this calmness was a reflection of strength. Thus, the painting became one of quiet strength—the dark muted tones and the powerful arm, lightly holding the work of art that he had carved.

I did a quick study of him and sketched in a 24 x 30 canvas with the blue t-shirt he was wearing. The second day he had found a black t-shirt with a white collar that he thought I might like better. Pazoom! I flew at the canvas, changed the composition, scumbled* in the dark tones, the head, hand and arm. The third day he announced that he could not come back and had to leave early. Everything had to go right; I said a prayer and jumped at the canvas. The paint flew, my concentration was never broken and when he had to leave, the painting was where I wanted it.

A short time after the sitting, Lyle had a very serious accident while fishing in the northern part of the province. He was incapacitated for some time and consequently had time to think about the important things in life. When I met him again in 1988 for an interview, he was working at the University of British Columbia Museum of Anthropology in Vancouver.

He told me that his family, especially his mother and his Uncle, Sam Robinson, were highly motivated and a positive contributing factor to his culture. During the early years

*scumble - painter's term for applying paint quickly

of Lyle's childhood, he lived with his grandparents at Butedale Cannery where he was born. He attended the elementary school at the reserve in Kitamaat Village, a school that housed four grades. He then went on to Kitimat town to complete grades 5 to 12. During grade 9, discipline had become a problem for Lyle and after all options were exhausted, it was decided to send him to residential school. A more disciplined atmosphere did not agree with him and he was back in Kitimat in three months.

After graduation, he worked for Alcan Aluminum for a year but eventually found his way to Vancouver, NITEP and the University of British Columbia. He transferred from NITEP to the regular university program for a degree in secondary art education. During this period, he became committed to teaching art and was determined to learn all he could, so he enrolled in the Emily Carr School of Art and Design in the printmaking program. On completing three years of printmaking he received his diploma in 1986 from ECSAD.

Gradually, Lyle found he was spending more and more time with his art than with anything else, and eventually it became his main purpose in life. The following is an excerpt of the Artist's Statement taken from the brochure "Lyle Wilson: When Worlds Collide," which accompanied an exhibit of Lyle's work at the University of British Columbia Museum of Anthropology:

" . . . Sometimes people ask me if I am an Indian artist. 'Yes,' I reply, 'I am an artist who happens to be Indian.' While my answer doesn't quite fit the question, I believe it adequately reflects my situation. I belong to a generation of Natives that was raised with a core of Indian values, and has to contend with the powerful forces which shape life in the twentieth century. Mentally these two forces first created a conflict in me, then a recognition of wasted energy, and finally a fusion of identities. . . ."

Lyle has successfully fused both modern influences and traditional values. This is evident in his art which is a combination of traditional Native art and contemporary, conceptual art and in his complex and compelling personality. His artistic goals are simple and straightforward: "I want to make the most of my abilities." His basic attitude in life is equally frank: "You be honest with me, I'll be honest with you, I have no time for mind games. My personal style is to learn about situations, analyse, then respond. Reason and logic are important to me."

Lyle's intense and sensitive personality makes him impatient with anything that impedes his progress and with those who do not measure up to his high standards and strong values. He pushes himself hard and expects nothing less from others.

. . .the colors that mean so much to her
people. . . .a symbol of harmony and balance

Painting #3
Size: 16 x 20 (40.64 cm x 50.8 cm)

Yvonne Dunlop (1950 -   )

Teacher

Although Yvonne Dunlop was born in Vancouver, British Columbia, she is a descendant of the Interior Salish L'ilawat Band at Mount Currie.

Yvonne is a graduate of the Native Indian Teacher Education Program (NITEP) at the University of British Columbia. She has taught elementary school at Alert Bay, British Columbia, and has worked with Urban Images, a program to help Native women prepare for the work force, and with NITEP as a counsellor and coordinator.

Yvonne taught me about the colors that mean so much to her people, the sacred circle, Mother Earth and about books such as *Seven Arrows, The World's Rim, Warriors of the Rainbow,* and *How Great Upon the Mountain.* It was the beginning of a great learning experience.

Yvonne Dunlop

In August of 1981, I did two paintings of Yvonne; one with a silver copper hanging from her neck and one that was to appear later in the series in brilliant blues, greens and reds.

During the sitting, Yvonne spoke of the colors which are very important in Native culture and which are situated on the Sacred Circle or the Medicine Wheel. These represent a system of organization where there is no beginning and no end, thus the circle. Within this Circle or Medicine Wheel, black stands for NORTH, red for EAST, yellow for SOUTH, and for WEST, white. These colors are also symbolic of the different peoples of the world and their different views of life. The Sacred Circle is a symbol of the interrelatedness of all things. The circle reflects the natural world, the cycle of birth, life and death; the sky, the sun and the moon, and the cycle of days and seasons. It also represents the wholeness of a person—spiritual, emotional, mental and physical. And it is a symbol of harmony and balance.

A letter from Chief Seathl (Seattle) written around 1852 to the President of the United States best tells how the Aboriginal people of this continent feel about Mother Earth:

"Will you teach your children what we have taught our children, that the earth is our mother? What befalls the earth befalls all the sons of the earth . . . This we know: the earth does not belong to Man, Man belongs to the earth. All things are connected like the blood that unites us all.

"Man did not weave the web of life, he is merely a strand in it. Whatever he does to the web, he does to himself . . . We love this earth as a newborn loves its mother's heartbeat. So, if we sell you our land, love it as we have loved it. Care for it as we have cared for it. Hold in your mind the memory of the land as it is when you receive it . . . As we are part of the land, you too are part of the land . . . No man, be he Red Man or White Man, can be apart. We are brothers after all." (Joseph Campbell and Bill Moyers, *The Power of Myth*, 1988, Doubleday, p. 33ff)

While with Yvonne I also learned about coppers, what they were, what they meant to the people, and how so many were confiscated after the Potlatch of 1922 when the Government imprisoned the participants.

It was later that I interviewed Yvonne and she told me of her home, her schooling, earning her teaching degree at NITEP and teaching in a reserve school.

Yvonne Dunlop Interview:

"I have a lot to learn. The teacher I admired and respected so much was an older woman; she probably retired soon after she taught us. She was so warm and caring. In the wintertime she would let all the dogs into the school, and they slept around the heater. That's the kind of school it was.

"I used to want to be a writer. When I was in high school, they would say 'what do you want to do?' 'I want to be a writer!' 'I mean what do you *really* want to do?'

"I have two daughters and a son; one daughter will be fifteen tomorrow, my oldest. She's working in Alert Bay, and my other children are visiting my mom. They had a soccer tournament up there and my son got a trophy; he got the first goal. We are newcomers to Alert Bay and everyone is into soccer so when my son got that goal, he was the hero.

"My daughter is also a goalie. She got a trophy for best goalie in the tournament. She was so shocked because that was her first tournament, her first year playing soccer. You could hear all these people clapping. They love soccer so much. It made me feel like crying. Well, it established her but she also got an award for the most inspirational dancer. She's a new traditional dancer in the Alert Bay High school; and my son got an award for the best all round academic student in the class.

"My father once said to me, 'I had a dream that you were teaching school in Alert Bay and that you were very happy!' That was in 1979, and so when I saw the ad for teaching in Alert Bay I phoned them, and they said, 'I'm sorry we are not taking any more applications.' I said, 'Fine, thanks, o.k., I understand. It's past May 25th.' Then the person on the other end said 'Tell me about yourself.' He interviewed me over the telephone and asked me if I would like to come up. That was one of the most interesting interviews I've ever had; all we did was laugh. Interviews are not like that, are they? As we came out of the office he said, 'We would like to offer you the job,' and that was my father's dream. When I tell people that they say 'Really? So, you came up here because your father had a dream?'

"I'm not the type of person that believes in putting your hand in and getting funding. I got funding from the University of British Columbia, but I went through school on student loans and I didn't get money from the Department of Indian Affairs or from my family; they couldn't afford it. I'm the type of person that really believes you are doing yourself a service if you go out and do what you want and you work hard for it and I don't believe in making excuses. If you really want to, you will do it. That's my philosophy.

"Indian people are really critical of the education system; their kids can't read, they can't write, and so on. I think they should be helping them. I think the parents should be sitting down and reading with them and playing reading games, and going down to the schools and asking 'Can my child become involved?' Let's not wait for other people to give money for some kind of program. Let's just do it!"

Yvonne laughed a great deal; I liked her very much.

A Journey of Discovery

. . . a story of reaching goals and going beyond.

After painting the three people who were to become the catalyst for *Chronicles of Pride*, I came across a textbook, used in the teaching of Native education, that caused me to explode. Looking up at me out of the illustrations were such brutally sad, distraught faces that I made up my mind then and there as to what I must do. I didn't realize the work I was undertaking; the years of constant research, speaking, administrating and eventually not having time to paint.

At first, I had to find people who represented my standards and satisfied my needs, with which I could make the statement that was growing in my mind. I spoke with a good old friend, Reverend Bob Faris, who had been on the "Thomas Crosby," the United Church boat which had gone up and down the West Coast of British Columbia. He and his wife Celia had eventually been posted to Bella Bella, a reserve on the Inland Passage, difficult to get to and difficult to leave. It had been an experience of such spiritual value to them, they hated to leave when the time came. I told Bob of my plans, and of course he knew many people who embodied the concept of the Native Indian which I wanted to present— one of strength, quiet determination, participation and contribution.

I visited with Saul Arbess, at that time Director of Indian Education, Ministry of Education, British Columbia; Madelaine Rowan, Ethnologist, UBC Museum of Anthropology; and then, Brenda Taylor, Native Home/School Worker for the Vancouver School Board, and the ball really started to roll.

The minute I started speaking with Brenda, you could see the wheels start turning. She was ready with names, contacts, anything that would help me. As you will see, I painted Brenda Taylor; a project concerning contribution would never be complete without her.

. . . I painted her in the spotlight, caught
up in the emotion of the moment.

Painting #4
Size: 24 x 28 (60.96 cm x 71.12 cm)

Margo Kane (1952 -   )

Actress

Margo Kane is of Cree descent, born near Edmonton, Alberta. She is an actress, singer, and dancer, who has taught the dramatic arts throughout British Columbia. Margo has made films and commercials in Canada and the United States. I painted her as if she were in the spotlight, caught up in the emotion of the moment.

Margo Kane

Margo Kane was in the process of organizing an all-Indian theatre arts group. She had just completed a movie, *Running Brave*, with Robbie Benson and was preparing to go north to give a workshop in acting and dance. I painted her on February 11 and March 16, 1983.

I knew the colors of the canvas would have to glow with her vitality and the brush strokes would have to signify her animation. I posed her as if she were in the spotlight, for performance is her life.

Margo Kane Interview:

"Well, I wasn't raised on a reserve with a band. I am Métis. My mother gave me up for adoption to my aunt and her husband, and I grew up playing outdoors a lot, running through the fields and forest. I love the outdoors.

"I was raised by non-Indians. I was Indian. Well I knew; I had known for years, but it was really a hard fact to face. I feel very much that it was my choice to identify with that part of my blood line because of the spiritual nature of the Native Indian.

"It was still a private joy to be Native Indian. Every now and again I would be reminded that I was darker skinned and that I was, you know, different. When you're growing up, you experience prejudice anyway just for not being pretty enough, or for not having the nicest clothes, so it was just another part of that kind of stuff, so it didn't stick out. And things might have been different if I'd been in an Indian family that lived on the street; I might have experienced more prejudice.

"Well, since I was a child I was always singing and acting and dancing and telling stories. I was really good, as I found out. I realized that I had some kind of skill in dancing as well; coming out of high school I was not sure what I was going to do.

"I had a lot of problems with drugs and alcohol and peer pressure; and I was really terrified. So I thought, well, what do you have going for yourself? What's good about who you are, is there anything that happened in your life that was really quite special?

"The most special thing was my experience with dance. I discovered that I had this wonderful gift. I just started planning the goals. I just started going. It was hard. It was hard training; I was too old. I was nineteen when I started seriously training as a dancer. However, along the way I did learn; teachers did push me. People recognized my talent. I got back into drama, I got back into singing and learned all those skills needed to be a professional.

"When I got a job in the theatre doing *Rita Joe* I had to do research for my role and I really got into what Native people were experiencing. I went out and did my research on skid row and into social services and the foster homes. Then I became concerned by what I was seeing and I wanted to help, I wanted to do something; I wanted to encourage, I wanted to be part of the community.

"And that was a turning point in my life. I was invited to a lot of places to speak and to be with kids in group homes and things like that; that's where all the role modeling started and it just kind of snowballed.

"I really express my inner self through movement and through performing. I've been learning to work with groups of youth and by explaining who I am and what I've gone through myself, and how I've used my own talents and what I think is important, they have some idea of the number of ways to express themselves.

"The youth work I do is really important to me because in some ways it was really hard for me, and I know exactly what they're going through. I believe that I need to be the most productive I can be for myself, for my family, for the Native community and for the local community. All the work that I'm doing really comes from the heart; it's not there for distraction. You know, I think I'm really spiritually connected to what it is I'm doing. I'm true to my own spirit."

Through networking with friends across the country, Margo encourages Native people to become more accomplished, more progressive in their art, more defined in their guidelines of professional standards. She hopes to work toward a great Canadian Native Indian production.

During the painting of the portrait, she was constantly planning and thinking of what she must do within the next few days. Her young mind was very active. She spoke of fasting so that she might be more receptive to guidance in the work she was doing. The painting went quickly and on the last sitting day, on impulse, she brought me a gerbera daisy, one of my favorites.

*. . . the white bear in the background is becoming more
prominent and an aura is appearing around her.*

Painting #5
Size: 24 x 28 (60.96 cm x 71.12 cm)

Dorothy Francis (1912 -   )

Singer, Dancer, Storyteller

Dorothy Francis is Salteaux, born on the Waywayseecappo Reserve in Manitoba. Dorothy is a recipient of the Order of Canada. She was given this award for her efforts in keeping Native Indian culture alive during a time when few others were passing on Native traditions to the next generation. She has promoted the culture through her work in radio, television and Native dance. She is also a founding member of the Native Indian Friendship Centre. A profoundly spiritual woman living to serve others, Dorothy has been a frequent visitor to people in prison.

She is painted in the beaded buckskin of the Plains Indian, with sweet grass beside her. The big white bear begins to form at the left of her head, while two more bears march along behind her. Dorothy's name in Salteaux is Maqua Beak, meaning "bear."

Dorothy Francis

I had found out about Dorothy Francis through a book published by the Secretary of State called *Speaking Together*. She is a beautiful woman with spirit, laughter and love. Born in 1912, a Saulteaux from the Waywayseecappo Reserve in Manitoba, she was raised with a strong awareness of her culture.

In the early years, Dorothy worked on radio programs. She sang Indian lullabies, read Native poetry and struggled to keep her culture alive. She also did a television series on which she told children's stories. She taught crafts, dancing and legends in the schools, and once was invited to dine with the Queen of England.

Later, she would be recognized by her country, Canada, for keeping her culture alive. The Order of Canada was presented to Dorothy on April 19th, 1978; it was a tribute from her country, a way of saying thanks for a job well done.

After the first sitting, I was notified that Dorothy had gone to the hospital; she had suffered a heart attack. However, within four weeks she was back again sitting for me in her buckskin dress, a Plains costume with beautiful beadwork. I had exciting ideas about a more contemporary composition for the painting, but in the end the personality of the sitter reigned.

Dorothy Francis Interview, April 18, 1983:

"When the American astronaut landed on the moon, when he first put his foot on the moon, he said 'The eagle has landed.' It made news, it was in the papers, T.V., everyone heard about it. The Indians heard about it and they got excited. They remembered this old man, Sweet Medicine I think his name was, an old Indian prophet. He said when this happens there will be a big change for the Indian people.

"They [Native Indians] have been so, what shall I say, downtrodden and mistreated for so many years, they've lost their spirit. They were made to turn to Christianity, and the Christians were fighting among themselves, getting everyone confused. It was hard for everybody. There were all kinds of things introduced to the Indian people and it was no good, they were not used to these things.

"After the war in 1939, the veterans—my husband was a veteran—came home. He never drank before, but when he came home he liked his booze. When there was a pow-wow or a fiddle dance, a get together, these guys would pull off their coats and look for a fight with somebody. So we used to scramble home. There was no more dancing; it slowly died off.

"I see such a change now everywhere, in the south, in the United States, in Canada, in the Northwest Territories; I see it happening all over. There has to be a change for the world. I've seen it and it is improving slowly.

"We have to make the Indians realize they are important people. Sometimes they are afraid to say they're Indian and me, I say I'm Indian before I say I'm English. So there you are! I want to help the Native people if I can; help anyone in this world, Chinese, Japanese, East Indian, English, Scottish, Irish—so many people. We need a spiritual renewal—one mankind."

First sitting, April 18, 1983:

The painting is, as usual, governed by the personality of the subject. This woman is so loving, peaceful and spiritual that I cannot do the clever things (in paint) I had planned. They do not relate to her in any way. Even on the second sitting, the dress seems too much. I must soften it all in the next sitting. The two bears march behind her head, but a third bear seems to be appearing.

April 25, the third and last sitting:

There is only the face to finish and the beads to put in. An aura is appearing around her and the white bear in the background is becoming more prominent. The third sitting became a party. It was difficult to retain the spiritual side of her, but then her love of life was also a side of her that I wanted to portray. She looked coy, happy and beautiful, and I hope the painting is a mixture of all these things. It seemed imperative to put Dorothy's Indian name, Maqua Beak, on the painting, so that was done on the fifth day in my studio.

We keep in touch. Although Dorothy is in a wheelchair, she still speaks at many important functions, still visits the prisons and is asked to be the prayer speaker at many gatherings.

As Dorothy says, the traditional spirituality of the Native people is significantly high. Their involvement with their Creator is as natural to them as breathing, and it is this spirituality which has given them their endurance, their faith in a Supreme Being and their high regard for each other as individuals.

Much later, Dorothy told me the significance of the big white bear in the painting. The Shaman had come to work his powers over the expired body of her husband. Suddenly in the smoke of his fire the image of a big white bear appeared. The Shaman told Dorothy it was the spirit of the departed, and this is what had unconsciously appeared in the painting.

. . . respect for himself and respect for others.

Painting #6
Size: 20 x 24 (50.8 cm x 60.96 cm)

Louis Miranda (1892 - 1990)

Language Teacher

Louis Miranda was Squamish, born in North Vancouver, British Columbia. At age eighty-eight, "Uncle" Louis Miranda worked with a linguist to put the oral Squamish language into written form. At ninety years of age, he was still teaching the Squamish language four days a week at Norgate School in North Vancouver, British Columbia. He received an Honorary Doctorate of Laws (LLD) from Simon Fraser University for his work on language development and for his outstanding contribution as an authority on Coast Salish and Squamish history, culture, and language.

When I painted "Uncle" Louis in 1983, he was most cooperative. He was so determined to help me that he sat perfectly still, refusing a rest, and I had to madly paint him in two hours. This work is called a "primatura painting", that is, a painting completed in one sitting.

"Uncle" Louis was dedicated to the belief that all people are created equal, learning this from his father who told him to look neither up nor down at anyone. Through respect for himself, he respected others and was an inspiration to many people, young and old.

Dr. Louis Miranda

When I went to see "Uncle" Louis Miranda on April 4, 1983, he was then ninety years of age, and welcomed me warmly. We sat down in his kitchen and with his elbows on the table, his hands clasped and his great head thrown back, he began to tell me the story of his life. Although deaf, he spoke easily and readily about his parents and the early years, and about his values and beliefs. He told me of his father and mother, and how he had lived and attended school in Squamish although born in North Vancouver. It was there he learned the Squamish language from two *English* girls who also attended his school.

"I was raised to believe I should not look up, nor look down at the white man; that all are created equal, that all are children of God. I was taught to have respect for myself and respect for my fellow man. You have to get your education, because the foundation of life is education, love, honesty and respect and determination that you're going to do what is right."

His memory for dates and events was exceptional. As I set up my easel in the kitchen, he struck a pose and would not move nor take a rest, so I attacked the canvas and completed the painting in two hours.

I had heard about "Uncle" Louis (a name given to him fondly by friends) from Chris Kelly, an educator with the North Vancouver School Board. I was told this man taught the children of Norgate School the Squamish language. With the help of a linguist, he also created a dictionary for the language. "Uncle Louis" felt this was very important because the Native Indian languages are quickly being lost as the elders die and take the languages with them. It is only because of the attitudes and vision of a relatively small group of people that these oral languages are being preserved. For this contribution, "Uncle" Louis was recognized by Simon Fraser University and given an Honorary Doctorate at the age of eighty-eight in 1981. An article written on this expansive and loving man says:

"'Uncle' Louis has a sense of values that have remained constant throughout changing times. At ninety he is upright, strong and agile, with no telltale lines of age nor frailty of mind, spirit or body."

. . . She sat behind the bench, welcoming new citizens to her country.

Painting #7
Size: 20 x 30 (50.8 cm x 76.2 cm)

Marjorie Cantryn White (1936 -)

Citizenship Court Judge, Businesswoman

Marjorie Cantryn White is Nuu-Chah-Nulth, a member of the Ohiaht band from Port Alberni, British Columbia. She started her career as a practical nurse and then went on to be a founder of the Vancouver Indian Centre, the first woman on the Vancouver Policy Commission, an assistant in the Office of the Provincial Ombudsman, a Citizenship Court Judge, and a businesswoman. She has spoken to many groups, trying to make the public understand Native Indian people and the problems of integration. She believes the success of integration depends on the cooperation of both Natives and non-Natives.

She sat in her judge's robe, behind the bench in the Federal Citizenship Court, Vancouver, British Columbia, presiding over the court and welcoming new citizens to her country. This is the way Marjorie Cantryn White was first described to me. I wanted to portray this diminutive woman in a way that would show the relationship between her five-foot frame and the enormous accomplishments she has achieved.

Marjorie Cantryn White

I met Marjorie at a salmon barbecue at the NITEP (Native Indian Teacher Education Program) hut at the University of British Columbia, to which I had been invited by Bev Berger, the coordinator of the program. I was told that Marjorie was a Citizenship Court judge. I couldn't imagine a woman of such minute structure being a judge before a court—the thought fascinated me.

I have attended Citizenship Court and all the while I imagined petite Marjorie in the seat of the very tall judge who was presiding over the proceedings. I could easily have painted her in her robes behind the bench but she had gone on to do so many other things that I rethought my approach.

Marjorie left her village in 1956 to become a practical nurse. Somewhere along the way she was driven beyond her initial desire and went on to be a founder of the Vancouver Indian Centre and the first woman on the Vancouver Police Commission. She accepted a three-year appointment as a Citizenship Court judge and in 1980 joined the office of the Ombudsman as an assistant to Dr. Carl Friedman who was Ombudsman at that time.

Marjory Cantryn White Interview May 20, 1983:

"I was nominated by one of our own local members of Parliament who recognized my community work and community involvement, and the office of the Citizenship Court judge does state that any citizen can be appointed as a Citizenship Court judge. I didn't have a law degree.

"I have always felt that the public has to be aware of the Native Indian people in this country and certainly we [Native people] have had a great deal of resentment simply because of the treatment we have experienced.

"Having lived in Vancouver for twenty-six years and having met many families, I find a lot of the parents are products of residential schools and in those days we were absolutely prohibited to speak our language or practise our culture and so those in my age group lost their heritage at such an early age we no longer really understood our culture and why we were Indian—of a different race—so it's been difficult for a lot of those parents to really instill any kind of Indian pride in their children.

"There are many of our people who are going into law and the law of this land has been one of our greatest crosses, in that so many of our people have gotten into trouble. They are serving prison terms which, I am sure, a lot of them should not be, but because they didn't have lawyers to defend them at the time they broke the law, or supposedly broke the law, some of them are serving life sentences. And I at one point suggested that there should be a Royal Commission on those who are incarcerated just to find out how many are doing life sentences and the kind of legal counsel they had at the time they committed the 'crime'. Unfortunately, in this province or anywhere in Canada, they have absolutely no training of any kind for Indian youth.

"Last month I travelled to Seattle with five of our students from Bella Bella and attended an Indian youth conference. There were over a thousand students from all over the northwest state and they went into various workshops. They got into teenage alcoholism, suicide and its prevention, stress and the students, leadership skills and self-image; really encouraging the student to understand him or herself and to be proud of who he or she is. It was a heartwarming experience for me to have been part of all this and to see that American Indians are actually preparing their youth as future leaders. And we are not giving our youth that same kind of preparation today.

"While my girls were growing up and going to public schools in Vancouver and Burnaby, I taught them our culture and always made them aware of our culture. They have always had role models. I think their biggest role model has been my uncle, George Clutesi. He was an artist, a writer, a lecturer, an actor. He was always a high profile in their lives, and of course, they looked up to him and have used him as an example. They have listened to him talk at home and he has given his versions of the white people coming into Canada, and so through all of that, they have a lot of pride instilled in them and they have never faced any kind of discrimination while they were going to school. I suppose it was really because they understood who they were."

Marjorie Cantryn White, after returning to Bella Bella on a semi-retirement basis, has come back to Vancouver to continue her search for a better world for her people.

. . . he knew he would live . . .

Painting #8
Size: 24 x 30 (60.96 cm x 76.2 cm)

John Williams (1921 -)

United Church Minister

John Williams is a Haida from the Queen Charlotte Islands of British Columbia. He was ordained in the United Church at the age of fifty-four. John told me of his experience in his twenties when he had tuberculosis of the bone. His doctors had told him he would surely die. He said goodbye to his father who had been such an inspiration to him. Then he had a dream:

When he awoke from his dream, John knew he would not die.

The painting depicts the dream sequence: the stripes of blue, the belief; the mauve, the dream; and the red and gold the hope and renewal of life. After one short sitting, John was called back to Kitamaat because of a death in the family. The dream sequence was painted after John left. I borrowed a clerical collar from Reverend Harry Robinson, painted that in and with a photograph from John's wife, Liz, checked out my highlights and it was done.

John Williams is now retired and lives with his wife in Skidegate Mission on the Queen Charlotte Islands.

John Williams

Although he seemed a very reserved man, the first time I met John Williams, he told me in his storyteller fashion of a dream he had when he was in his twenties. He painted such a vivid picture of this dream that of course I was inspired to paint just that.

John Williams Interview, April, 1983:

"My grandfather was the son of a Welsh man who went to Nanaimo from Wales and married a Haida chief's niece. He was born in Nanaimo and when he was about eight years old, the uncles came down from the Charlottes and announced to the mother that they were taking their nephew, and that someday he was going to be chief. They said that parents were always too easy on their own children. They had left him until he was eight years old because they knew his mother and father loved him very much. From the age of five a child is trained in the duties and responsibilities of chieftainship.

"My grandfather grew up as a Haida chief's nephew. The mainland people called him a prince. He didn't take his name until he was about fifty-five years of age; then he took his uncle's name. He died when he was seventy-six.

"In 1938 my grandfather, John Williams, and a man named Luke Watson carved a canoe for the Museum of Man in Ontario and my grandfather died that same winter. I also wrote my high school entrance exam that year. The following year, 1939, the Inspector of Indian Schools saw my marks and on the basis of an eighty-six percent average he decided that he would not allow me to go to high school because I might turn communist. Captain Barry was the Inspector of Indian Schools for British Columbia; a Captain in the Canadian Army from the First World War. There was no political science then and apparently he equated good scholarship with communism. He had a phobia about communism, I guess the whole government had a phobia about communism; 1938 was the height of the Depression.

"In the autumn of 1939 I became sick—chest pain, bad cough. The doctor said that it was tuberculosis, so I went into the hospital and after two months, there was room at the Vancouver General Hospital and they shipped me down there, where I stayed in isolation until I left.

"In 1940 my bones began to crumble; my collarbone was broken nine years before when I was nine years old. The doctors said they could do nothing. In the tradition of my people, when a person is dying the ancestors and the dead relatives come twice a day usually; they come to fetch the dying person in a canoe. At high tide, they take him and they go home. The doctor sent for my father to come see me for the last time because I was dying. When he went home he was convinced that he would never see me alive again.

"That night I dreamed that my grandfather was coming across the Skidegate Inlet in the canoe that he and Luke Watson had built. He was coming to take me hunting on the west coast. I was lying in bed in the hospital in Vancouver, but in my dream I was back in the Charlottes, sitting on the front steps of my father's home.

"It was a beautiful summer day, right on the horizon there was a deep blue, almost black, eastern horizon; the sun was setting, the tide was high and above that it merged into deep purple, then mauves, then various reds lighting into orange where the sun was going down. I was facing east. When the canoe landed, I grabbed my father's rifle and ran down the hill.

"There's a little creek separating the village and the beach; when I reached the creek I remembered that there was no ammunition for the rifle, so I called to one of my cousins, he was about six or seven years old. I said to him, 'Simon, tell grandfather that I can't come this time, I have no ammunition; I'll come next time.' He ran cheerfully down the beach. Then I went back to the house dragging my feet feeling sorry for myself because I couldn't go. I watched my grandfather as he paddled back toward the west coast; I could hear him singing the eagle paddling song. He wasn't worried; he had all the patience in the world, there was no hurry.

"When I woke up in the morning, I told my father, don't worry about me any more, I'm going to be all right. When the doctor came to see me on rounds that afternoon, I told him I wanted him to operate, either scrape the bone or remove it, get rid of the collarbone; so he removed half of my left collarbone together with the joint that holds it onto the shoulder.

"There was no exercise at that time; there was no such thing as physiotherapy. I think that came after the war or during the war. So I just relied on one nurse in the Indian Hospital at Coqualeetza in Sardis. She told me to put my elbow on my knee and push my hand with my other hand. It used to feel as if my joint was breaking but I persisted in doing it. Her name was Marilyn Harrison.

"When I went home I used that therapy as much as I could. Eventually I regained full function just doing things instinctively. I used to watch animals that had broken a limb and I watched how they handled it, so I knew that it was necessary to use it before it felt right. I started to use it without consulting the doctor; strength came back. I only have half the strength because there is no collarbone.

"They were convinced that the Indian Affairs would put me on disability for the rest of my life. I went home and five months after that, about a month after recovering from double pneumonia, I went fishing with Harry Martin, the toughest fisherman in the Queen Charlotte Islands. He was stone deaf and ninety-two percent blind, and he taught me about commercial fishing. He was my father's first cousin. The year after that I got my own boat and went trolling for a total of fourteen years.

"The Indian way of dealing with people is to respect each and every individual. I was taught this from childhood by three woman who lived in both cultures: my great aunt, my grandmother and my great-aunt on my mother's side. The people who respect themselves must also respect other people.

"My great aunt said ancestors were picked so that the children would never surrender in battle, they died fighting rather than become slaves. And she said you couldn't cry no matter how hard you tried, you couldn't cry, unless it was for a loved one who died. Then she chuckled.

"'It didn't always work the way we wanted it to,' she said. 'We would take the family that was getting too timid, too gentle, and we'd marry them into a family that was getting so cranky that you couldn't even look at them without getting something thrown at you or being hit. Instead of being somewhere in between half of them would be so mean that you couldn't talk to them and the other half would be so gentle that they would burst into tears if you looked at them the wrong way. But in the long run,' she said, 'it worked out the way we wanted it to.'"

While sitting, John spoke of his father a great deal; a man who must have been a great inspiration to him. He spoke of his schooling and the fact that he had to resort to fisticuffs at times to defend himself. I was amazed to find that this quiet man had studied karate! That inbred strength and courage came to the fore many times in John's life—when he was a child of small stature and later when he was a young man.

At the time he was painted, his parish was in Kitamaat village. He has since retired and he and his wife Liz have gone to Skidegate Mission to make their home. In his contribution as a man of God, he doesn't believe in preaching; his philosophy is to provide gems to ponder, and allow people to find their own answers.

(Stories - permission of John Williams)

. . . Glen allowed me to paint the inner man.

Painting #9
Size: 20 x 24 (50.8 cm x 60.96 cm)

Glen Newman (1944 -)

Band Counsellor, Social Worker

Glen Newman is Squamish, born in North Vancouver, British Columbia. At the time of painting in 1983, Glen was a Squamish Band counsellor and administrator. He has held the positions of reserve social worker and Native consultant for the Ministry of Human Resources.

I believe Glen's love and concern for people and his response to life make him an outstanding humanist. In the painting, I have tried to make the viewer aware of this man's outgoing personality through the use of paint and brush work around his head and shoulders and the expression on his face.

Glen Newman

I was discussing this project in the office of Brenda Taylor when Glen Newman phoned her. As soon as she had hung up the receiver she said, "Glen's name is the first I'll give you." I contacted Glen and we were in business.

I have wondered many times how the people involved with *Chronicles of Pride* could give me an unknown quantity of their valuable time. They all came to my studio two or three times, sometimes four, and sat and told me—someone they didn't know—their innermost feelings. I could not believe it at all, but I listened, never hesitating. Those who could not come to my studio, I painted on their reserves. That was to be another experience!

When I met Glen, I was immediately aware of his personality. After talking together awhile, he said to me, "You're doing this from the heart; you are bound to make it work."

Glen Newman's attitude toward life is positive. His love of people, which shows on his face, and his desire to help his people is the essence of the painting. I feel he is an outstanding humanist.

Life is always a learning process; and while involved in painting this series, I gained greater understanding of attitudes in Native Indian culture. For example, the traditonal Native family is an extended family and within this group, Native children are often raised by relatives who are not the true parents. These mother and father figures are always loved and respected whether he or she is the natural parent or not. Painting Glen was the beginning of this new understanding and it was his open nature that helped me.

When you are painting someone, the quality of the work is often related to the communication between the sitter and the artist. That communion allows the artist to depict the inner man. If the artist and subject do not communicate, the artist must look for another approach to the portrait. Glen allowed me to paint the inner man.

On June 1 and June 6, 1983, Glen appeared early in the morning, in time to eat breakfast with my husband and me, and then we disappeared into the upper regions, there to catch in living color the Glen Newman who was emerging from our conversations. We covered many topics and I found that "Uncle" Louis Miranda had touched the life of this young man. It appeared that Glen had been turned on to war canoe racing through the intervention of "Uncle" Louis. While many of his peers were getting their excitement from less strenuous and more debilitating activities, "Uncle" Louis urged his young friend to continue his schooling and to become involved with the traditional sport of Native culture. This interest that began when he was fifteen has continued for twenty years.

Glen Newman Interview, June, 1983:

"He put the canoe blood into me when I was fifteen. Instead of boozing it up, taking pills, he got me into canoes. That's why I say he is my inspiration for discipline and sportsmanship.

"I guess I was one of the first Native social workers. I worked in social services in Vancouver for two years; they gave me the hard cases or cases that they felt I could communicate with.

"When I was sixteen I had feelings for people, I don't know where it came from, but on the reserve I had seen a lot of my cousins going to jail, Indian boys the age of sixteen and seventeen being charged with mischief. So I have seen a lot of pain on the reserve. One of my brothers died from drugs and my younger brother went to jail for eighteen months for breaking and entry, first offence. He just turned seventeen, but he got a year and a half, so I don't know, I just had a feeling that I wanted to do something.

"I was forced into school, so I struggled through the whole school system. I struggled and did all my homework. Education was sort of a second civilization; it wasn't home ground.

"One of the things I noticed when I worked in the city was the lack of spirituality among the professional social workers. In my personal and professional experience, I find that 'society' assumes everyone has the same values. These values, set down by 'society', are materialistic. When social workers are helping in the Native community they must realize they are dealing with different standards and values, which are more personal. I think maybe it has changed a little now, but I remember that lack of spirituality toward human relations. With a client there has to be feeling; there has to be empathy.

"My biggest concern was children. They were being apprehended left and right. I checked the statistics; there were 536 Indian children who were in white foster homes in Vancouver alone, in 1976. I was very shocked. I worked for the Vancouver Children's Service in 1968. I quit and came back to the reservation. I was asked to go back on the reserve and set up some social development programs."

Through Glen's involvement with social work on the reserves, he sees the need for our two cultures to work seriously to gain an understanding of one another, with the emphasis on the spirituality of all people.

. . . His son, Junior, had gone to the podium to receive the honor.

Painting #10
Size: 24 x 30 (60.96 cm x 76.2 cm)

George Manuel (1921-1989)

Politician

George Manuel was born on the Shuswap Reserve in British Columbia and was a member of the Neskainlith Band. George was a politician and had an active career as president of both the National Indian Brotherhood and the Union of British Columbia Indian Chiefs. He united Indigenous people all over the world by forming the World Council of Indigenous Peoples. For this work, he was awarded the Order of Canada and received an Honorary Doctorate (LLD) from the University of British Columbia in May 1983.

When I was with George and his family during the sittings, I found him to be a warm, cooperative, personable man. I tried to show these qualities in the painting. George encouraged me greatly in my endeavor to portray the Native Indian people and their contributions to society.

George Manuel

A nother relationship that held great pleasure for me was the one with George Manuel. To me he was a gentle, family man who became a good friend. He was a man of empathy who encouraged me in my endeavor. George was a well-loved politician—loved by those who followed him, held in awe by those who opposed his platform.

He lived in Aylmer, Quebec, while working in Ottawa as leader of the Indian National Brotherhood, and travelled to many countries with ministers of portfolio, as the Native consultant. In this capacity, he came in contact with Indigenous peoples throughout the world and became their champion. He has had an illustrious career—Grand Chief of the Union of Indian Chiefs; founder of the World Council of Indigenous Peoples; honored by the University of British Columbia and honored by his country.

He came for two sittings. He was easy and relaxed, and talked of many things. Sandy Charlton, a friend and a photographer, took pictures while we talked. George was not well at the time. He had been unable to accept his Honorary Doctorate at the University of British Columbia in July 1983, and his son Junior had gone to the podium to receive the honor. George was making frequent trips to his doctor and came for sittings after appointments. His wife and three children brought him; we would all have lunch together and after the sitting they would return to pick him up.

George Manuel Interview, July 5 and 14, 1983:

"Well I would like to talk about my childhood years on the reservation. The vision of my life at that time was limited to riding horses, and of course we were experts in canoes; interior small canoes was the mode of transportation we were using at that time, canoes and horses.

"When my father came back from the first world war he had been gassed and so he had one hundred percent pension, and was totally useless physically; he was gassed badly. So the first thing I remember in life was going to live with my grandfather and I travelled with him through the mountains, fishing for trout.

"When I was about twelve years old, I started to be with other young people the same age as me, and we had an orchestra, a western orchestra, but we never could raise enough money at that age, so somehow that dream passed.

"I met Dan George and his family when they came up into the Interior from Burrard Inlet because that is where he was born and raised, and they wanted a holiday and they didn't have any money. We were really extremely poor, the thing that I remember of my life, our lives I should say, is the poverty."

George and I went out on the porch for some air, and he told me that in the early years he had been a farmer, sowing seed for distribution, and then Buckerfield's, a seed and grain distributor, moved in and monopolized the market. To discover how a thing like that could happen, he turned to politics. It was the beginning of his political career.

"One of the things that entered my mind was that Indians are strangers in their own country. There's nothing written about the Indian people in the textbooks. There are no historical records, no textbooks about the history of Native people except the very negative aspects. This painting gives a totally different perspective.

"There has to be more education in politics and nationalism in schools, I think. That's where it starts. Dancing, beads, bannock and stuff like that, that's not culture. Canadians in general are the same; they have a shallow outlook of what a nation is about. Native Indians don't fit any categories politically. We have failed to identify and move onwards; to design a philosophy, collectively, that will express our ideals for our own tribe, band or nation.

"You have to be mature and you have to be a nationalist. I don't think Indians understand what nationalism is! They have a long way to go. Our short term goal has to be survival—making sure our kids get enough education, food, good health and proper homes. They have got to understand and make their minds work. They just pursue old lines, old schools of thought; they have to have new lines of thought and ideas.

"I made a speech in Peru about three years ago and I had an audience of about 15,000 Indian people, and I told them that we have to have our own ideology. We don't fit into the Right and we don't fit into the Left. That's why we are fragmented completely; we are always on the losing end, the deprived end of the stick.

"That was the first time an ideal was ever proclaimed in Native culture. Now that the idea has come it's talked about in many parts of the world, but there is no movement, just talk. I'm proud that I introduced the idea."

George's final comment in the interview emphasizes his strong belief that the Indigenous peoples of the world should work together to develop a common economic and political theory. He believed they must have a united belief so that in that strength they could rise and be heard. If George Manuel's health had not given out he would, no doubt, have pursued this dream.

George Manuel died in November 1989.

. . . The energy and vitality must be contained in a few brush strokes and I must pull them out of the air.

Painting #11
Size: 24 x 24 (60.96 cm x 60.96 cm)

Gloria George (1942 -)

Lawyer

Gloria George is Gitksan Wet'suwet'en and was born at Telkwa, British Columbia. Gloria George has been involved in the administration of Native Indian programs at all levels: planning, researching and lecturing. She has served on the Human Rights Commission, the organizing body of the World Council of Churches, and the Board of the Canada Council. At the time of the portrait sitting in 1983, she was in the second year of her studies to be a lawyer. She received her degree in 1990.

Gloria is very focused, intelligent, and intense. Her attributes suggested an intense painting, so with a light directed onto her face and a limited amount of brush strokes, I worked toward that feeling.

Gloria George

The experience of painting Gloria George became an emotional one for both of us. An artist, especially a portrait painter, must be aware and open to all there is to see, hear and feel. The intelligence, earnestness and intensity of Gloria suggested an intense painting.

> The intelligence swings like a pendulum before my eyes and I must capture it on the swing past; The energy and vitality must be contained in a few brush strokes and I must pull them out of the air.

The interview with Gloria George, on October 8, 1983 was one of the most interesting and informative tapes I did. Among other things, she felt very strongly that the word Native must be eliminated. "These people are Squamish, Capilano, Haida, Kwagiutl, etc., and we must learn to differentiate as we do with Scottish, English, Welsh; otherwise they are Canadians or Aboriginal Canadians—aboriginals indigenous to Canada."

When the painting was done in October and November of 1983, Gloria had done part of her law degree; since then she has completed her studies. I feel like shouting, "Look out world—here comes Gloria George!" This latest addition to her long list of achievements is just the beginning.

Gloria George, outstanding administrator and involved citizen, has lectured, presided, researched and planned. She was a guest on *Front Page Challenge* on the James Bay Agreement, and as a director of the World Council of Churches Sixth Assembly, went around the world gathering Indigenous people for the assembly held at the University of British Columbia a few years ago. In this account of the experience of Gloria George, I must include some of her thoughts.

Gloria George Interview:

"There's a difference between functioning and surviving. We survived—now we want someone who can function in both worlds. What's discouraging is our educational system and the information that is fed to the general public is still so limited, and as more and more of the Indigenous issues come into focus publicly now, many of the communities still do not understand Canadian Indigenous history and its positive contribution. And I guess what upsets me sometimes is that the majority of the people I work with are totally unaware of Indigenous history and still see me as a stereotype; and I am categorized that way.

"I have achieved not only beyond my individual potential, I have achieved beyond the community's potential, and this was to emphasize that there are very strong, positive, intelligent contributions I can make as an Indian descendant. And that was the only way I could establish credibility. Our Indigenous communities still are not in the state whereby they can receive their own educated Indigenous people back; Indigenous people who go out to be educated become so educated it makes it very difficult for them to return to the Indigenous community.

"The Indigenous community is fighting for self-determination, and self-government. Self-government has to come about by recognizing the contributions of those Indigenous people who are trained and specialized and also who are professionals, and they have to be integrated back into the Indigenous community.

"Many of our Indigenous males are married to non-Indigenous women and so there is a conflict of spiritual and material values. These values are not synonymous. Spiritual values are all-encompassing; materialism leads to greed.

Many men are employed in the industries such as forestry, mining and agriculture; they were in the World Wars and thereby lost their land and the natural resource base. Now away from their traditional territories, they marry out of their Aboriginal community.

It's very hard to come out of the residential school system and remain attached to the traditional extended family in these mixed marriages. They have been divided legally, physically, psychologically, and there lies the difficulty in the melding of the two cultures.

The Indigenous community has to be educated in the professional sense. They have to be taught how the community functions and how government, bureaucratic and corporate structures feed into it.

"The word 'Indian' is no longer really applicable although some people will identify Indigenous people as such because of the Indian Act, but the Indian Act is going down the tube anyway. Columbus made the error of naming Indigenous North Americans 'Indian', and we should recognize that in Canada we have a multicultural society and there are Indians here and those Indians are from India. They've immigrated to Canada much like the English and the Scottish and everybody else.

"There is a group in B.C. called the *Native Sons of British Columbia*; and there is certainly no Indigenous population in that association. And there's also a group called the *Native Daughters and Order of Native Daughters*—well, they're descendants of the British who happen to be born in Canada, so the word native has no tribal affiliation whatsoever and the word Indian has no relationship whatsoever other than Columbus' error.

"There's a lot of non-Indigenous people who are willing to support Indigenous issues and we just have to utilize their strengths rather than scattering them. I think the text of your book should keep saying Aboriginal and Indigenous all the way through, because your book is there to educate people. Get away from the context of Native and Indian. Those two words just no longer apply.

"The churches had a huge influence on our population and on creating the legal division; and now I think the churches are trying to right their wrongs. I don't think they'll ever right their wrongs because too much damage has been done; but many church people are committed to drawing Native peoples' *issues* into their fold, not drawing us into their fold. They are now recognizing our Native spirituality as a separate, whole living thing. It's a whole livelihood, our native spirituality, it's not a one-hour on a Sunday thing. I'm not a one-hour Christian—I'm a 24-hour Native spiritualist."

. . . He stood seven and one-half feet tall.

Painting #12
Size: 26 x 34 (66.04 cm x 86.36 cm)

Simon Baker (1911 -)

Band Chief, International Native Representative

Simon Baker, an elected chief of the Squamish, is a member of the Capilano Band in North Vancouver, British Columbia. Simon has been an inspirational chief and has done much to enhance the living conditions of his people. After living off the reserve for many years, he returned to it in order to push for simple, but essential, amenities like proper electricity and running water. These accomplishments earned him the respect of the Native community. Simon Baker has travelled as a Native ambassador to Germany, the Netherlands, and Japan.

In the painting, Simon wears the costume of the Plains Indian. The costume was given to him by the Plains people and is worn when Simon represents the North American Indian in countries around the world.

Simon Baker

When Simon Baker stood up in my studio he reached seven and one-half feet tall in his headdress and Plains costume. The top feathers bent backwards on the ceiling of my painting space, dwarfing everything around him, an impressive sight.

He chooses to wear the beautiful buckskin costume when the airlines send him around the world as a public relations figure representing the North American Indian, and this is what he believes the world wants to see. On his arrival in Germany, he is met by large groups of people arrayed in the finest Indian costumes who belong to various Indian associations.

The existence of North American Indian "clubs" in Germany no doubt stems from the great number of books written by Karl May several decades ago about the adventures of a tribal Indian and an old prospector. German children have been raised on these stories and have developed great empathy for the North American Indian. Each year there is a Karl May festival in Bad Segeberg and Espe to celebrate this writer of true fiction, who had never left his homeland; all the stories were written from his imagination.

Simon did a great deal to enhance the living conditions of his people and is looked upon with great respect. In his youth he played lacrosse with his brothers and cousins for the "North Shore Indians" (an imposing figure even in his youth). Lacrosse is a game handed down through the Indian Nations and while Simon and his siblings took part in this strenuous and sometimes hostile exercise, good sportsmanship was always the rule.

During this time, Simon lived in the "white man's world", but later chose to go back to the reservation. He took with him knowledge of the things he had experienced; better living conditions such as hot running water, proper heating, inside conveniences, electricity and sanitation. He wanted these things for his people and worked toward creating a reservation which gave them the humble decencies of life.

Simon Baker Interview, August 26, 1984:

"I am from the Capilano Band. The Capilano reserve is one of the many bands situated on the north shore and we have sixteen reserves in our band. We are known as the Squamish tribe. The government came along and gave us all the land that they felt we needed and the land they gave us they called 'reservation'. We were given twenty acres to each one in a family.

"We're all baptized in the Catholic Church. We know it's the truth. We know my grandfather was a dedicated Catholic. When he moved he built another church on the Capilano Reserve, a beautiful Catholic church. They asked the Bishop to come and consecrate it, bless it. He wouldn't come. Nobody would. So that church was built; it stood there.

"The church was never used and stood there for years. I tore that whole big church down by myself, salvaged all the good lumber, everything. I built my first home down on the waterfront out of that church. That was one of my first projects and it was quite a nice home. In those days the families always liked to live together. Well, you can imagine about seventy people living in one house. We always had a full house.

"My grandmother used to go to Vancouver in the old days. She would row in the canoe across the narrows right into Vancouver where the old immigration building used to be, right down at the foot of Granville Street. And she used to go up to the west end, sell her baskets, berries, eggs, whatever she had, twice a week.

"She was an Indian princess from birth. She witnessed the peace that they had with the northern Indians; she was there to witness the gathering of all the different tribes when they settled. There would be no more fighting, no more stealing and taking slaves.

"Khotlacha [man with a kind heart], so am I recognized in the whole Indian society—Vancouver Island, all the way up north. Wherever I go now the people will ask me to sit right in front. If there's anyone to speak at any big gathering, I am always the first one. They ask me because I come from the mainland and I'm recognized as one of the leaders of our people from the past.

"I once told my grandmother 'I want to go to the white man's school.' I wanted to further my education; I felt that I could do a lot, I wanted to learn more. I was quite an athlete too. I used to box, wrestle and play basketball. I played with all these guys. When they grew up they all settled down, went through university. A lot of them became doctors, lawyers, real estate, you name it.

"After that I got married, settled down, I joined the Council of the Squamish tribe. We had close to a million dollars in our capital fund that was derived from the sale of land and timber; the government wouldn't let us touch it. All we got out of it was the interest that was distributed among our people every Christmas. We were lucky if we got fifteen dollars each.

"There was nothing we could do because we did not have enough people in the Council that had much education, much experience. I told them, it's time we did our own thing, so we formed a committee. When I got through with the Indian agent, we got over four hundred thousand and started building our sewers, and putting hot and cold water in the houses. The agent said to us, 'If you use that money you aren't going to get your interest.' Ten or fifteen dollars doesn't give us enough money to improve our homes.

"Today we have one of the richest reserves in Canada because we went ahead and developed it, we have a good revenue coming in, and we run our own affairs; we have our own administration."

Simon has shown pride in his heritage by making the most of life in his own way. With dignity he has represented his people around the world. For Simon's ambassadorship, he received an Honorary Doctorate of Laws from the University of British Columbia on May 29, 1990.

. . . a man of great vision, insight and compassion

Painting #13
Size: 24 x 30 (60.96 cm x 76.2 cm)

Vivian Wilson (1924 -)

Fisherman, Entrepreneur

Vivian Wilson is Kwagiutl from Bella Bella, British Columbia. At the age of sixteen, Vivian Wilson bought his first boat for three hundred dollars. With determination and integrity, he built a Pacific fishing business which now involves three generations of the Wilson family. This business includes Coastwide Fishing, a small fish processing plant which ships fresh salmon and herring roe to Japan.

Out of concern for his people and in response to medical emergencies that have arisen, Vivian Wilson also built a Native Indian airline named Waglisla. This airline transports the people of Bella Bella, Alert Bay, and other small coastal villages to Vancouver, where they can get special medical attention. Waglisla Airline now services Alert Bay with a direct flight from Alert Bay to Vancouver as its next goal.

Bob Faris told me about Vivian and about the great contribution he was making to his people. As I added up the numbers of men and women, young and old, diversities of vocations, I added him to my list. We met and went on from there. The sittings were on June 6, October 4 and 11, 1983.

The painting shows Vivian's plane—a vision which has become a reality.

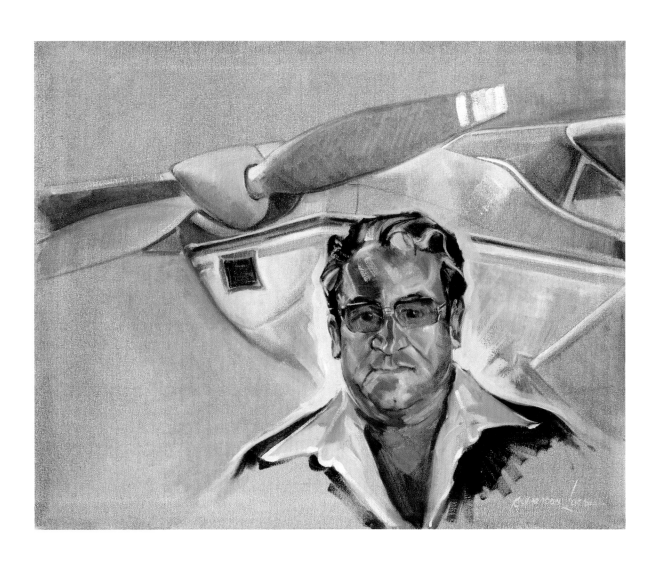

Vivian Wilson

Bella Bella, situated on the Inland Passage on the west coast of British Columbia, was cut off from medical services when significant emergencies arose. When Vivian Wilson told me of his decision to build an airline into Bella Bella and the smaller communities, I chose to paint him with his aircraft behind his head as a vision. He had begun as a fisherman when he was a young boy with a three hundred dollar fishing boat. He built a reputation of stability and quiet determination. With this behind him, he developed the all-Indian airline, "Waglisla" that would transport his people to the hospitals in Vancouver.

Vivian Wilson Interview, October, 1983:

"I flew up to Ocean Falls. From there, I had to charter a plane to get to Klemtu. Those people are so isolated. This friend of mine told me about the licenses that were available and I looked into it. It was a chance to help those people in Klemtu. We're doing a big service there. We got our license from Air BC; they are the carriers but they're not servicing those areas.

"In the future, once we get our licenses, we're going to try and get into Rivers Inlet as well. We want to help them get a new airstrip. It's essential to get them to hospital. Our plane goes up there sometimes but you have to go up-river and it's pretty dangerous.

"One of our pilots is John Waterfall, Pauline's husband. We have two Beavers, a C-185 and hopefully an Otter by next year. I've been fishing for forty-five years; have a sixty-five foot seiner. I let my partner run the airline—I'm a fisherman."

Before the sitting, Vivian had an accident while flying into Bella Bella in a very small float plane. It flipped upside down and Vivian, strapped into his seat, hung suspended beneath the water. The people of the village came to the rescue, and so Vivian was preparing for his second potlatch. The first had been for his brother-in-law who had been a chief, and the second would be to give thanks to the people of Bella Bella for saving his life.

. . . when he wears the eagle feather, he must walk tall.

Painting #14
Size: 24 x 36 (60.96 cm x 91.44 cm)

Leonard George (1946 -)

Actor, Film Producer, Band Chief

Leonard George is a member of the Coast Salish Burrard Band, Burrard Reserve, North Vancouver, British Columbia. He is a founder of the Dan George Memorial Foundation, which promotes Native culture through film, television, radio, and other media. He is himself an actor and producer of films and videos dealing with Native Indian culture and is often asked to perform Native dances and songs at functions for dignitaries visiting Vancouver. Leonard is engaged in a personal quest. As a recovered alcoholic, he speaks in his quiet way to the youth of today about the destruction caused by alcoholism and urges them on to better things. Leonard George became band chief in 1989.

Leonard told me that when he wears the eagle feather, he must "walk tall". I painted him in the Coast Salish costume that he wears when he sings and dances—the little wooden paddles on his tunic making a mellow, clacking sound as he beats his drum and whirls in dance.

Leonard George

I heard Leonard George sing a lament at the service held for Blanche Macdonald at the time of her passing. The haunting strains filled my heart with longing. The very large group of friends, acquaintances and loved ones sat quietly with tears streaming down their faces. We were moved to another time and space.

This young man, an exceptionally talented Native singer and dancer, had sat for me the previous year. We had two sittings for the painting: April 24, 1983 and May 14, 1984. In the painting he stands tall, beating softly on his drum, wearing the eagle feather.

As I painted, Leonard spoke: "A drum is really the heartbeat of Mother Earth. It is used for entertainment at weddings and get-togethers of many kinds, but always has its spiritual contribution—it fits in well with the wheel of life. The wheel of life is designed after the earth itself.

"The earth has to be balanced by north, south, east and west; and we should also, in order to be in balance with the earth. Therefore we are to look after ourselves in four directions. Those four directions are physical, mental, emotional and spiritual. Singing and dancing allows you to look after yourself in all ways. You are using your physical being, relieving emotions related to mental stress, or dancing because you are happy, and the drum evokes spirituality."

I was hearing some of the same things that Yvonne Dunlop had told me at the very beginning of this journey. Leonard opened his heart to me as he does to the children and youth to whom he often speaks. He tells them of the time when he was not caring for himself in the way he had been taught and how he'd lost everything through alcohol and drugs. He tells them how he'd ended up with nothing but a bottle and an empty house.

A priest started working with Leonard, nagging him, following him, getting under his skin and finally convinced Leonard to enter the treatment centre that eventually helped him. After much discouragement, soul-searching and finally prayer, Leonard started on the long road back to humanity. Since then, Leonard, with his family, has been a never-ending reminder of the spirituality of Native Indian culture through his dancing, singing, acting and the founding of the Dan George Memorial Foundation.

Again he spoke to me: "I can remember before I'd go to sleep, I'd be just lying there looking out the window. I would lay in my bed and look straight out the window over the inlet and just start crying for no reason really. I remember my mom talking to me about it and she'd ask me, 'What's wrong?' I'd say, 'Well, what can I do? Right now, I feel so helpless. What can I do to help my people?' And she'd say, 'You can't do anything right now. But you can—you will in time.'"

Education has been the very essence of Verna's life . . .

Painting #15
Size: 20 x 24 (50.8 cm x 60.96)

Verna Kirkness (1935 -)

Educator

Verna Kirkness is Cree and was born on the Fisher River Reserve in Manitoba. It was in high school that Verna first questioned what it was to be Indian. She has worked diligently in the area of Native Indian education and believes that Native Indians must know and understand themselves. If she can help to accomplish this and work toward society's knowledge and understanding of the Indian people, she feels the progress that follows will affect all Canadians in a very positive way. The Kirkness Adult Learning Centre in Winnipeg was founded in Verna's honor and she is the Director of the First Nations House of Learning of which she was a founder.

My first impression of Verna was of a cooperative, intelligent career woman. When she arrived for her sitting for the portrait, I was also struck by her femininity. I quickly decided to paint her in a much more delicate way—more like a watercolor. I had arranged for three sittings but did a semi-monochromatic on a 20 x 24 white canvas in one sitting.

Verna Kirkness

At the time the painting was done, Verna Kirkness was the Director of the Native Indian Teacher Education Program (NITEP) at the University of British Columbia. Since then she has been Director of Indian Education Administration at UBC, and is now Professor Kirkness, Director of the First Nations House of Learning. A school has been opened in Winnipeg in her honor, the Kirkness Adult Learning Centre.

I had spoken with Verna at NITEP. She was very cooperative and took time from her extremely busy schedule to be a part of *Chronicles of Pride*. She impressed me as being serious and formal, but when she appeared for her sitting away from the offices of the university, she was relaxed and casual, and I realized that I had to rethink my approach to the portrait.

I like to have several canvases prepared for these spontaneous decisions. An artist must have faith in his or her intuition and "carry on". There are always several ways you can envision the subject to be painted and you must decide on one—and as I say, "carry on".

Education has been the very essence of Verna's life. When she was a very young child, the door to the schoolroom was something she attacked with enthusiasm and excitement. She pleaded constantly to be allowed to go to school but, alas, she had to wait until she was the right age; a difficult task for the determined little girl. If her mother needed her at home, she would cry and carry on to such an extent that her mother would finally succumb; and Verna was off to school—her first love. Throughout her life, she has shown that same determination in her work for Native education.

After grade twelve, she and a friend decided to take a six-week crash course instead of going to normal school and got into teaching right away. In her first job, her oldest student was fifteen and she was eighteen.

Verna explained the problems she faced: "I was one of the few Native teachers in my province in those early times. I guess I can consider myself privileged to have been able to work in all these areas, always breaking new ground. I was quite young then. I'm still quite young.

"A northern school division in Manitoba wanted me to take care of education for all of northern Manitoba, including non-Indians. But they were also in charge of some federal schools, some Indian schools and also a number of Métis communities. So I went there and I was their first supervisor. I was like an inspector. They had two hundred teachers and I was the only supervisor. And they were all isolated. You had to fly to a lot of places. So it was all crisis oriented. I just had to go where the problems were."

She continued along this course throughout her life, flying into the far north, breaking new ground, developing new courses, acting as teacher, principal, curriculum consultant, education director and finally freelance consultant. She worked with governments, universities and Indian bands evaluating their school programs. She started a National Indian Research Association—a body of graduate level Native Indians from across Canada with a mandate to research Indian education.

An Institute of Native Studies at the University of British Columbia? Tom Berger and Verna Kirkness co-chaired a committee to look into how the University of British Columbia might assist the Native people of the province both on campus and in the community; thus, the First Nations School of Learning.

On May 11, 1990, Verna received a honorary degree from Mount St. Vincent University, Halifax, Nova Scotia. A Doctor of Humane Letters was presented to her for her work of over thirty years for Native control of Native education.

To quote Verna "In a nutshell, education has been my whole life."

. . . the gift of "choice"

Painting #16
Size: (30 cm x 36 cm)

Paul Willie (1944 -)

Laboratory Technologist, Band Manager

Paul Willie is Kwagiutl. He is one of the four hereditary chiefs of Kingcome at Kingcome Inlet, British Columbia and is band manager. At the time of painting, he was head of the Bio-Chemistry Laboratory at the Royal Columbian Hospital in New Westminster, British Columbia. Later he became head of health services at Alert Bay.

Paul lives comfortably within both cultures. He taught me many things about the oral history and the philosophies of his Native culture.

Because, as an artist, I love the challenge of painting white smocks, I was delighted to find Paul at work at the hospital, standing beside his blood machine. The use of a toned canvas gives clarity to the subject.

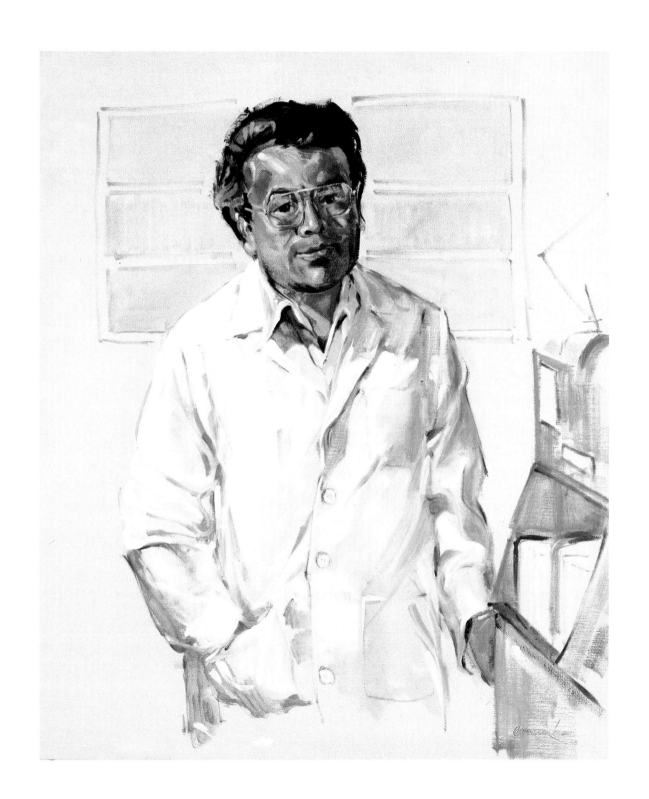

Paul Willie

Paul Willie had been suggested to me by a mutual friend and when I went to see him on March 7, 1983, at the Royal Columbian Hospital in New Westminster, I was delighted to find him wearing a white lab coat. I always wanted to paint someone in a white lab coat; I don't know why, an artist's whim I guess. There was also a blood machine in the background that I could work into the painting, and would add some vibrant color.

I learned much from Paul. He explained that the history of his people was handed down through stories, and one of the stories was about the Great Flood, which shows his ancestors go back a very long time, 10,000 years. He told me, "The greatest gift given to the Indians by the Creator was the gift of 'choice'. What you do with your life is your own choice and one thing is not above another.

I also learned about potlatches, and after painting Paul, I went to the Museum of Anthropology and saw the film *Potlatch*. It helped me to understand what happened to this important part of West coast Native culture and the effect it had on many people of that culture. In the film, I also saw Agnes Alfred for the first time, who I would later paint.

Paul Willie, a Kwagiutl, was born in Gilford which is on the northern tip of Vancouver Island, and belongs to a tribe called Datowadeno. He is hereditary chief of one of the four tribes of Kingcome. As a laboratory technologist Paul works in an urban location confirming diagnoses by physicians in hospitals. On the other hand, he lives his traditional culture as a chief in the village of Kingcome. This man lives comfortably within two worlds.

Common sense and an open-minded philosophy of life are some of Paul Willie's attributes. Paul believes the problems of Native Indians have to be faced and that you must make the best of what you have.

Paul Willie Interview:

"We have to live in this world regardless of what happens. Certainly what has happened is very important, but what is equally important is how we *react* to what has happened. I think people who have had bad experiences in residential schools should look at part of them as character builders, not pitfalls. You have to hold on to the past and you also have to evolve. You have to adapt to the flow, not necessarily go with the flow. I think it is important to be able to live and adjust, and yet keep your sense of identity.

"I believe that we are of the spirit world. We enter the physical world and when life ends, we again enter the spiritual world. It is a complete cycle. When you enter the physical world you are certain to be given choices. The path you choose is your choice. You can be a victim of circumstances, but then you have that choice as to how to cope with that situation.

"To make our separate societies work together in harmony we have to learn to understand our differences and not grade our differences as being good or bad, but accept them for what they are. I find people only listen and hear what they want to hear, but I go on an individual basis, finding out what makes people tick and hopefully expressing what makes me tick. I believe that birth is part of the growth of the spirit, and the spiritual body is more important than the physical body. Some believe that, some don't; but like I said, we all have our differences.

"Self-government—are we really ready? It's like a double-edged sword; will we ever be ready or do we just go and swim and see what happens? There are a lot of problems to iron out before our people can truly enjoy self-government. I think we have to unlearn what we have learned from the white man—to rely too much on a politician's point of view. On the reserves in British Columbia, the people in control are out for themselves. This is a sad thing. We have to learn to treat people a lot better.

"The traditional concept of a chief is someone who is willing to love and serve his people. That is the ideal way, but nowadays politics enter into it; one group working for you, one group working against you. We can no longer live the way we did before the White man came. Those days of hunting and fishing are gone for everyone, not just for the Indians!

. . . earth tones and a fleur-de-lis

Painting #17
Size: (30 cm x 36 cm)

Blanche Macdonald (1931 - 1985)

Entrepreneur

Blanche Macdonald was Métis. She was born in Faust, Alberta. Blanche was the founder of the Blanche MacDonald Modeling School and Career College in Vancouver, British Columbia. She helped many women develop a feeling of self-worth that enabled them to enter the work force with confidence. With the help of Mel Bevon, she also established Native Communications in British Columbia. This broadcasting system carries radio programs to Native communities throughout the province.

I painted Blanche as a handsome model, because she was a role model to so many people.

Blanche died June 8, 1985.

Blanche Macdonald

I had contacted Blanche Macdonald about being part of my series, and she was very open to the idea but we had great difficulty in making time for the sittings. She was either leaving town or speaking somewhere: "Let's wait for a month or two when it's not so busy . . ." After calling a dozen times, I decided to forget Blanche.

An artist must have a preconceived idea of what the composition of the portrait or painting will be so that a canvas can be prepared in advance. I had never met Blanche nor had I seen a photograph of her. I had really given up on catching her when without conscious thought I had a notion of how I would paint her. I wanted her in a black dress with a big white collar, earthtones in the background and a fleur-de-lis somewhere, probably floating around her head and, oh yes, her hair had to be short. I called her once more, it must have been the fourteenth time. She said she would come that night and we started the following Saturday, January 21, 1984.

To my great surprise, she appeared at the door as you see her in the painting, wearing a black dress with a big white collar. She had recently renewed her Métis ties, which are symbolized by the fleur-de-lis, and oddly enough her hair was short—a coincidence? The "image" of Blanche Macdonald was what I wanted to present in this instance, rather than her inner being, as it is the image by which she is most widely known.

I interviewed her at her sun-filled home in Deep Cove, British Columbia. The meeting was moving and memorable. She enthused about her home town of Faust, Alberta, and the people she grew up with, and how they had all made something of themselves.

In the school of learning which she founded, she prepared women for the workforce by encouraging feelings of self-worth and security. She had worked with many races, many stations, many ages and few were aware or cared that she was Métis.

During the sittings, we had long talks over elegant lunches. And through these congenial conversations, I gained some insight into the life of a woman who fought for the survival of her people, even though she was completely accepted in society.

Blanche had a very positive image to her credit and the credit of her people. She is missed, but if what Paul Willie says is true her spiritual life has evolved through her time here on earth. In 1985, at the memorial service held for her, the many hearts which she had come close to were gathered together to pay their last respects to a woman who had done so much for so many.

There have been many articles in the newspaper about Blanche since she passed away, and I agree with one writer as to how unfortunate it is that so often we stop and find words of praise the person deserves, only after their passing.

*. . . within a very short time accomplished a
goal beyond her imagination*

Painting #18
Size: 18 x 24 (45.72 cm x 60.96 cm)

Peggy Shannon (1943 -)

Teacher

Peggy Shannon is Haida from Masset, on the Queen Charlotte Islands of British Columbia. A grandmother at forty and determined to overcome alcoholism, Peggy decided to upgrade her education. First she completed her secondary education, then she attended the Native Indian Teacher Education Program and received her Bachelor of Education from the University of British Columbia. She also received a Master's degree at the same university. Peggy has used her training to teach basic education to Native adults. She has also turned her attention to an entirely different field and has used her artistic ability to craft earrings in the Native style.

I hadn't met Peggy before she arrived on January 25, 1984, but she suited my scheme of things and came with a strong recommendation from Verna Kirkness, Director of NITEP. I had planned on an 18 x 24 canvas, upright, and would use light to make my statement. Fortunately she wore a turquoise dress. I used my favorite cerulean blue and sat her right beside the studio window with the corner of the room disappearing behind her into the shadow. Her strength of character was depicted by her strong features, the intensity of color in her dress and the electricity of the space around her.

Peggy Shannon

Peggy Shannon is also from the NITEP program at UBC. She did extremely well in her studies and it was suggested that she be included in my series. I was looking for people who had set goals in their lives, surpassed obstacles, reached their goals and gone beyond. I was looking for a balance of men and women, young and old and from various walks of life. Peggy met the criteria.

At thirty-five years of age she was a mother and a grandmother. She made up her mind that she wanted an education so she upgraded her secondary education, went through NITEP to receive a teaching certificate; and then, she decided she should get her Master's Degree, went to UBC, and within a very short time accomplished a goal beyond her imagination.

Peggy, like many, had been devastated by the residential schools and had an incredibly difficult time dealing with the experience. Residential school robbed her of her identity, her feelings of self-worth and her ambitions. Now she had burst forth and soared with the eagle.

She told me a tale of struggle and deprivation. Only strength of character and purpose could have given her the determination to do what she has done. From an alcoholic background she has journeyed far. Her contribution to the education of her own people will be one that holds great weight and her participation in this series, as a role model, will be a valid one.

Peggy's goal as an educator is "to make people aware of a more positive lifestyle of the contemporary Native Indian, more positive than they now presume to be true." The thing that gets behind Peggy and pushes her along is "the desire for a betterment of Native communities as a whole." Her rebellion against the nightmare experiences of her youth has taken the form of a positive contribution, and she has become an example for many.

*. . . I did a quick study of the head
and let the surplice flow.*

Painting #19
Size: 20 x 40 (50.8 cm x 101.6 cm)

Matthew Hill (1946 -)

Chief Counsellor, Lay Reader, Fisherman

Matthew Hill is Tsimshian, from Kitkatla, British Columbia. He is one of the hereditary chiefs of both the Eagle and the Blackfish tribe. When the painting was done in 1984, he was the chief counsellor of his village, lay reader in the Anglican Church, and skipper of a thirty-eight foot fishing boat. He and the other fishermen in the village shipped herring roe and kelp to Japan. Matthew Hill has since moved to Prince Rupert and has been elected president of the Tsimshian Nation and president of the Native Brotherhood in Prince Rupert.

Because of the variety of Matthew's responsibilities, I had a choice as to how I would portray him. Here again was my opportunity to paint "the white smock", so I chose to show him as the lay reader of his church, leaving much bare canvas in the process.

Matthew Hill

Matthew Hill was introduced to me through a mutual acquaintance. When I heard of the strength that had made him an exceptional chief counsellor, a progressive fisherman, a lay reader of the Anglican Church and the devoted father of three, he was added to my list.

On February 29, 1984, Matthew was in Vancouver for a special meeting and I had to catch him in the evenings and work fast before he went back to his village. The mutual acquaintance obtained a surplice and cassock for him; I did a quick study of the head and let the surplice flow. The painting was completed in the one sitting—two and a half hours (five hours total working time), while John Robertson interviewed Matthew.

Reverend John Robertson of the Anglican Church approached me with Matthew's name. He had been active in the village of Kitkatla, British Columbia on Dolphin Island, 50 miles northwest of Prince Rupert (population about five hundred) and felt that I should include a Tsimshian by the name of Matthew Hill.

The Tsimshian live in the area south of the Skeena River area, west of Tweedsmuir Park, north of Klemtu and east of Browning Entrance Strait—all Tsimshian nation. Matthew's father and grandfather had been strong leaders of their community and he was expected to follow in their footsteps. Matthew is Chief Counsellor of the village and through hard work, dedication and I am sure by example, a good working exemplary group has been established.

The village grows kelp beds in which they harvest herring roe and this is shipped to Japan. The villagers are fishermen, descendants of those sea otter and fur otter fishermen who lived at the turn of the century.

Matthew is the skipper of a thirty-eight foot fishing boat called "Island Brave" and he has incorporated his fishing business, Matt Hill & Sons. In the capacity of lay reader he visits the elders and the sick, and so comes in regular contact with all the villagers.

"I attended junior high in Prince Rupert, and then the senior high until grade eleven. Then in grade eleven, I guess I was still wavering as to what I would do with myself, what I would make of myself. So my uncle and aunt suggested that I go to the Okanagan [namely Naramata] to take a six month course there in lay training. That was a good experience for me. I was about twenty. I have been the lay reader for thirteen years. I also got involved in the Church Army, a branch of the Anglican/Evangelistic portion of the church. I assist the parish priest, John Martinson, in his services and in visiting homes."

Matthew as a father, with his father's hat on, was concerned about the education of his children. He was torn between two responsibilities; his children and his village. Neither route could be taken without great deliberation, for Matthew is a man who accepts responsibility and wears it well. After the painting was finished in 1984, Matthew moved his family to Prince Rupert because of the greater education opportunities there for his children.

. . . We listened to many accounts of a man of dignity and good humor.

Painting #20
Size 28 x 34 (71.12 cm x 86.36 cm)

Alfred Scow (1927 -)

Judge

A Kwicksutaineuk, southern Kwagiutl, Alfred Scow was born in Alert Bay, British Columbia. He is a member of the Gilford Island Band. Judge Scow was called to the bar in 1962, which made him the first Native Indian to be called to the bar in British Columbia. He was sent by the government to serve on a land commission in Guyana to study the Amerindians of that country. At the time of painting in 1984, he was presiding over the Provincial Court in Coquitlam. Then he became Roving Judge for British Columbia.

The robes of a Provincial Court Judge are colorful and I chose to paint Judge Scow in a manner that underlined the dignity of his position.

Judge Alfred Scow

At the invitation of Gloria George I had gone to the testimonial dinner for Judge Alfred Scow, held at the Vancouver Indian Centre. We listened to many accounts of a man of dignity who also had a great sense of humor. The Honorable John Fraser, MP, who had been in law school with Alfred, spoke along with many well-known personalities, including Chief Simon Baker.

As the first Native Indian to be called to the bar in British Columbia, Alfred withstood the barrage of jesters at the dinner with his crinkly smile; and the warm words of camaraderie with more difficulty. It was a hilarious yet moving evening. I met the Judge's wife, Joan, and told her I would be contacting her husband in the near future.

Judge Scow Interview, March 21, 1988:

"My mother is the daughter of the chief of Fort Rupert and her mother was from the chief's family of the Nimpish, but our home reserve was at Gilford Island, that's where I spent most of my growing up years, from the time I was born until I was nine years old. Most of the time, our lifestyle was governed by fishing. I don't remember much of those early years except that there were many communal houses or big houses on the reserve, and at least nine longhouses then in the village.

"For a few years during the spring, summer and early fall, there were only two families living at Gilford Island, the Fords and the Scows. Part of the time there was the Coon family, so the Scow and Coon families were the only survivors of the Bella Coola massacre that took place before the turn of the century.

"According to my father, one of the people from the families stole a ceremonial whistle from the Bella Coola and they found out about it and they didn't do anything about it until the potlatch was finished.

"The Bella Coola went home and consulted with the rest of the tribe. They decided the crime was great because this ceremonial whistle was apparently a very sacred instrument to that particular family. They decided to teach these people a lesson, so they came in the night and killed just about everybody, but some members of the families ran into the woods and some were part of the families that were away camping or at another village.

"One young man was taken by the Bella Coola as a slave. He was from Kingcome and was visiting our village and he happened to be the one they took. And so they raised him as a Bella Coola and when he came of age he was told who he really was. He worked in camps and canneries and when he heard about the railroad that was being built in Prince Rupert he went there to get work. He worked on the railroad until he made enough money to go back home. The whole process took thirty years.

"One of my happiest memories when I was growing up before I went to school was moving about the waters of Gilford Island in my canoe. My mother had a small canoe that I used because my father was away a lot. So I would cut down an alder and trim it into a spear and drift down the inlet to the shallow water with my spear ready, and when I saw a fish I would spear it. I also collected crabs, and had my private little island that I used to row over to. It was about two hundred yards from the village and because it was a smaller island behind a bigger island, the whole village was out of sight."

Judge Scow remembered the many difficulties at residential school:

"The schooling in the mornings followed by heavy work in the afternoons; the strap across the leg if you were overheard using your own language; the harsh discipline when we were used to family love; the constant reminder of our inferiority and paganism.

"We used to have movies every two weeks in the early part of my schooling at the residential school and we often had cowboys and Indians. As children often do when they are together, we re-enacted some of the more dramatic scenes of the movie and of course, we played cowboys and Indians. Everybody wanted to be a cowboy; no one wanted to be an Indian. The trauma of those times caused psychological blocks for many, but then many rose above it all and accomplished much in their lives."

Guujaaw, a hunter and gatherer of food . . .

Painting #21
Size: 24 x 36 (60.96 cm x 91.44 cm)

Guujaaw (1953 -)

Hunter and Gatherer

Gary Edenshaw demands to be known by his Haida name, Guujaaw which means "drum". He is a Haida from Masset, on the Queen Charlotte Islands, and traces his ancestry to Skedans.

Having a quiet, but forceful character, Guujaaw works tirelessly for the preservation of his ancestral homeland of Haada Gwaai (the Queen Charlotte Islands) through writing articles and involvement in many of the political confrontations of his people. Also a dancer, singer, carver, and carpenter, he embodies the spirituality and pride of the Native Indian people. He has been called upon many times by Bill Reid, a well-known B.C. artist, to assist with the carving of Reid's projects.

May 31, 1984: "I see the painting clearly now. His strength comes from his spirit and his belief in the land and it's treasures. The spiritual side is strong and he is very content to be called a hunter and gatherer of food."

June 4, 1984: "He had brought a beautiful blanket vest with a hawk design on it. In one and a half hours it was all roughed in."

June 10, 1984: "We went out to the shed and painted for four hours. The painting went through a wild stage, then a mischievous stage and finally settled down to that proud, strong, yet vulnerable image."

Guujaaw

One of my subjects suggested that I paint Gary Edenshaw because he commanded so much respect from his peers. He was at that time carving a canoe with Simon Dick, Native carver and dancer, in the carving shed at the University of British Columbia. I spoke to him on the phone and went to see him on May 12, 1984. He is a handsome young man and is very much aware of his physical and spiritual strength. I had to overcome that force, and yet that force had to be in the painting for it was a part of him.

Guujaaw posed for me beside the carving shed with the sunlight coming through the trees. His quiet sense of humor made the sittings enjoyable. He was standing with his heavy axe in his hand, as he wanted to be known as a hunter and gatherer of food. He also most defiantly wants to be known as GUUJAAW, not Gary Edenshaw—GUUJAAW!!! (a potlatch name meaning, drum).

Guujaaw's proud stance in the portrait says much about the Haida. He is a descendant of warriors who sailed sixty foot war canoes in the deep waters of the Pacific. They rowed down the west coast of North America to distant lands and went on raiding parties to take slaves of less fortunate tribes home to the Queen Charlottes. Guujaaw has been among the staunch champions of Lyell Island, standing in the front row singing and beating his drum—sending the message clearly that he and his brothers and sisters are ready to protect the land they love.

Guujaaw is a carver and a carpenter—a man of many talents. Although he spends time on the lower mainland working with Bill Reid or on some other project, when he is on Haada Gwaai he lives a very basic life, drawing his food from land and sea. He uses the resources of both to live the traditional life.

He writes well about things he knows best. Many articles have appeared in the media about him or written by him. He has also published a book, *The Cedar* (Vancouver Wedge, 1984). This describes the creation of a totem pole, from choosing the tree, to carving and erecting the pole. If you have met Guujaaw, you won't forget him. Neither will you forget the painting of him. He is a young man of strong will and indomitable spirit who firmly believes in himself, the land, and his way of life.

. . . *there he was, younger and leaner than I had imagined.*

Painting #22
Size: 28 x 36 (71.12 cm x 91.44 cm)

David Gladstone (1955 -)

Dancer, Native Historian

David Gladstone is a Heiltsuk from Bella Bella, British Columbia. He is a link between the old and the new. Through respect for the elders and his extensive knowledge of local history and language, he has earned the right to wear and display the traditional costumes he has collected, and to perform the songs and dances of his people. These costumes are displayed in a museum in the secondary school at Bella Bella. Through his work as a language teacher, David has further helped to preserve the culture of his people.

Together David and I chose the costume he wears in the painting—a Chilkat blanket that he designed and his mother made, an apron with pounded pennies and quarters that jingle while he dances, a conical hat, and a clapper in his right hand.

David Gladstone

I had been told about David Gladstone and how much he was contributing to the community. I received a most interesting letter from him on June 14, 1983 and proceeded to make my plans. I had also contacted Pauline Waterfall from the same village and although she couldn't understand why I wanted to paint her—being an unassuming person—she also agreed.

The trip to Bella Bella on June 29, 1984 to paint David Gladstone and Pauline Waterfall is one I won't ever forget. The flight alone was an experience of a lifetime. We went up in a DC-3, one of the most beloved planes of former times. I heard someone call it a "bucket of bolts" and say that the last time it landed in Vancouver the cargo door fell off, and on take off it had trouble holding its wheels up. Whether any of those remarks were true or if it was just a joke between two DC-3 enthusiasts, I don't know, but it didn't help me at the time!

From my seat on the port side of the plane, I couldn't see Bella Bella, only the beautiful shoreline of that inland passage. Suddenly we were landing. I looked out and saw rock, gravel and wilderness; the gravel was about the size of tennis balls. A flat area fell away less than twenty feet on either side of us—this was the landing strip.

When we disembarked, all we could see were the vast areas of barren rock and scrub. There was a bus waiting as we taxied in. The pilot helped with the baggage, and before we left for the village we stayed to watch the plane taxi to the end of the "runway", do a death-defying turn on the edge of the world and take off. We were the ground crew! The bus driver radioed Vancouver that the plane had taken off and that he had thirteen passengers on board; and we were on our way.

The water in the puddles splashed through the floorboards right up onto the passengers. There was a doctor from Toronto aboard, along with his wife, who had come to British Columbia for a month to serve at the hospital in Bella Bella, and I thought they must have felt they had come to the "wild, wild West."

We had a long water taxi trip and then there was David Gladstone waiting for me on the dock—younger and leaner than I had expected. He took me by cab—I use the term loosely—to the place where I was to stay. I had been offered the home of the local teacher.

David and I walked through the village getting to know each other, discussing which costume he would wear (there are many) and planned to start painting in the Darby Memorial church the next day at nine. David stood, sat and slept on the floor while I painted, and in two days the details of his beautiful blanket were in place. He designed the Chilkat blanket he wears. His mother spent a year making it, his Aunt Florence made the apron, Aunt Peggy the leggings, and the hat is too old for anyone to know who made it. The rain poured down the whole time I was there, but the people I had come to see were warm and friendly and I enjoyed it all, including the delicious salmon that David's mother cooked for us.

David is a quiet spoken, serious young man who smiles easily. He speaks thoughtfully and well. He has a great love and respect for the elders, and for the young. I have the feeling that David is loved in return.

Bella Bella, situated on the inland passage, faces many problems. All commodities in the village are very expensive as everything has to be shipped in: bread, $2.50/loaf and shingles to fix David's roof cost $90 for shipping, just to come from Ocean Falls.

Because the village uses wood almost exclusively for heat, there are many fires. For safety, David's collection of songs, dances and costumes, which is of great importance to the community, will be placed in the Museum he plans to build in the well-appointed high school.

David Gladstone represents the growing interest of young Natives in their heritage. At one time, villages, determined to adopt the ways of the white people, denied their own traditions. This route led to much unhappiness and loss of identity. By learning the language and other aspects of their culture, David and others are preserving the valuable heritage of their people, promoting respect for their culture and enhancing the lives of Native people and others.

. . . she spins mud into fine pots.

Painting #23
Size: 24 x 30 (60.96 cm x 76.2 cm)

Pauline Waterfall (1944 -)

Teacher

Pauline Waterfall is Kwagiutl from Bella Bella Reserve, British Columbia. She is descended from many chiefs on both her mother's and her father's side of the family.

Pauline made a valuable contribution to her community by holding classes for adults wishing to raise their level of education. These classes were held at the secondary school in Bella Bella.

At the time of painting in 1984, Pauline and her husband lived on a houseboat on the outskirts of her village. This was because Pauline had lost her Native Indian status when she married outside her culture, and therefore, was not legally allowed to live on the reserve. The passage of Bill C-31 has rectified this for Pauline but not all non-status women have been as fortunate.

Pauline is an avid potter, so in the painting I showed her on a stained canvas, as a potter spinning mud into fine pots.

Pauline Waterfall

When I first heard of Pauline Waterfall from Bob Faris, I thought, what a beautiful Indian name. It turned out that she is married to an Englishman with a beautiful English name! When I contacted Pauline in June, 1984, she said she would work with David Gladstone to arrange accommodation for me in Bella Bella.

On July 1, 1984, Pauline sat for me in the school where her potting wheel is housed and where she spins mud into fine pots. We talked as she sat at her wheel and I applied paint to a stained canvas. She spoke of her adult students, about the way she felt about clay and her craft, and how she lived on a houseboat at the water's edge because she was a non-status Indian. Although she comes from a long line of chieftains, one of the most prestigious families of Waglisla (Bella Bella), she can't own a home and live in her village because she married a non-Indian.

Pauline Waterfall Interview:

"In essence, I was an outsider in my community. I applied to lease a lot so we could pull our floating home up on land but it did not come to be. We wanted to go on the land because of our five-year old son. He's fallen into the water three times and we've almost lost him. On one occasion I didn't even know he had fallen overboard. There was a man; he was the only other person down at the harbor. He was down there pumping his boat . . . and he saved Brett. It was a very sobering experience."

Pauline spoke of her grandmother who is a great influence in her life, and her great-grandmother, Yilistis, who died when she was ninety-six years old.

"When I knew that she was dying [Yilistis], I did a family tree, because it was such a large family. I was interested in knowing how extensive it was. At that time she had 396 direct descendents, certainly the matriarch of half of this village. I've been very interested in researching as much as I can about our culture, because I think it's important to know our roots. Whenever we have potlatches I do research on the family histories and I share it with the people who are giving the potlatch.

"My culture is fascinating to me now that I'm at this stage in my life. I think the thing that fascinates me about my people is that they are so innovative. They adjust so readily and they cope so well.

"I think that Bella Bella became less self-sufficient as more modern conveniences were introduced. The less conveniences we had, the more we had to rely on nature. The more distractions; the less cohesive we became as a community.

"I worked at the local college. I was hired as a tutor and worked there for four years. I taught business courses to eight women who were re-entering the work force. I tutored a social studies course to an upgrading class of six adults, one of whom is a grandfather, by the way. In September, we enrolled a man who was totally illiterate—one of the most exciting challenges of my life. If I can only succeed even a little bit, then it is all worthwhile."

I finished the painting in the one sitting and before I left, Pauline had phoned her aunt, Nellie Starr in Kispiox, my next stop, and arranged for me to stay with her while I painted Walter Harris. For a few days, I became the extended family of Nellie and Freddie Starr.

Walter and I walked down to the encircled area that houses the
old totem poles of the ancient village of Kispiox...

Painting #24
Sized: 18 x 40 (45.72 cm x 101.6 cm)

Walter Harris (1931 -)

Artist

Walter Harris is a hereditary chief of Kispiox, Gitksan of the Kildu people. He was born in Kispiox, British Columbia.

Walter is an artist of distinction, who carves masks, totem poles, boxes, and bowls. His totem poles are situated in many places, including Baltimore, Maryland; San Francisco, California; and Rochester, New York. His carvings enhance the doors at the House of Commons in Ottawa. At the time the painting was done in 1984, Walter Harris was teaching carving at K'san near Hazelton.

I painted Walter before his family pole, which sits in Kispiox by the mighty Skeena River. When Walter showed me some of his carvings, I was particularly impressed with one mask on which the eyelids opened and closed.

Walter Harris

As the bus drove through the devil's paintbrush burning red, the Queen Anne's lace as big as saucers and the daisies tilting their heads this way and that, I tried to imagine what my next subject would be like. Twice I'd heard his voice, and I conjured up an image to go with the voice. I wondered if it would be close to my imaginings. New Hazelton was the next stop—then on to Kispiox and Walter Harris.

Kispiox, British Columbia, is a beautiful part of the country. The village lies alongside the Skeena, quiet and serene beside the river's turbulence. Here the fish are caught, lives are lost, the water rushes and tumbles—truly the "Mighty Skeena". This is where Nellie and Freddie Starr welcomed me.

The view from their porch was a painter's paradise and while I devoured the surroundings, the whole family gathered to can the fish which Freddie had brought home. There is a job for each member of the family down to the youngest child. Survival is a natural instinct and everyone participates in the struggle for existence.

Walter and I walked down to the encircled area that housed the old totem poles of the ancient village of Kispiox, and he showed me his family pole. I had prepared a long narrow canvas with the image of Walter and a pole in mind. I decided to paint him standing in front of the family pole.

I am a direct painter and spend little time in preparatory sketches unless I am uncertain of my composition and want to feel my way. It is more necessary when a complicated composition is required, and when there are areas which need "discovering".

Walter told me about teaching at K'san, the village whose construction is based on Indian philosophy. K'san was built on the site of the old Gitksan village and was in fact a traditional replica. In the Gitksan tradition the head chief had the largest longhouse in the centre of the area, then other chiefs built on either side according to their leadership position in the community.

ancient poles in Kispiox

The village of Kispiox is an ancient one and some of the remains of it lie there among the wild flowers where the flooding river has taken its toll. The derelict houses, filled with ghosts of past lives, sit calmly and serenely telling quiet tales of happier times. This quietness pervades the character of Walter Harris, and his quiet voice and quiet ways complement the warmth of his face.

Walter Harris Interview, June 7, 1984:

"I was working in Rupert all winter and then I was out fishing all summer, so I decided to come home and stay home with the family, and it just happened that there was a night course in jewellery, so I got talked into it by my wife and sister, and I got really interested in it once I got going. I was working at K'san helping construct the buildings there. So after I was finished and school started, I decided to give it a try. After a couple of years, I gave up fishing and I just put my carpenter tools away and got into the art. I've never really picked them up since.

"I started putting out good things and people started to notice. Victoria put that 'Legacy' together around 1971 I think. They were buying everything that was good. It's all at the museum and they tell me that it's still mine. At the Museum of Man in Ottawa, people like George MacDonald and Bill Taylor gave us a lot of promotion through *Arts Canada* and art magazines, and then we got a big commission from the Royal Bank which really gave us a lot of publicity. That was the first big commission. Well, I've worked all over the country since then. There were quite a lot of pole commissions . . . San Francisco, Baltimore, and some smaller ones sold all over the country. I enjoy doing them.

"I do a little bit of stone. I got a commission from the federal government to do a stone for on top of the door of the Commonwealth Room in the House of Commons. Well, I just wanted to do one mask with the eyes that move. I always try to do something that moves, that's kind of a Gitksan style of mask. It took a bit of work to get the eyeballs to fit though.

"I've been teaching students how to make masks, poles, rattles, and then they do a small pole. I've been teaching the second year course, the advanced course. K'san has done a lot of good for different people. We teach people from all over the province. I'm building a workshop and I'm hoping to have all kinds of programs going there once I get going on it. The schedule will have to be fixed so that I don't have to teach day and night."

I spent very little time with Walter as the painting went so quickly. His wife was in Vancouver and I had upset the household enough. I was always aware that all these people were giving me their time and I hated to take advantage.

Since then Walter has suffered a stroke—unfortunate at this point in his career. I know he will persevere so that he can return to his art. I wish Walter well.

A man of Liberal persuasion . . .

Painting #25
Size: 28 x 36 (71.12 cm x 91.44 cm)

Len Marchand (1933 -)

Senator

The Honorable Len Marchand is Okanagan, born on the Okanagan Reserve in Vernon, British Columbia. He is a member of the Liberal party and was elected a Member of Parliament for Kamloops/Cariboo in 1968. He was only the second Native Member of Parliament, the first being Louis Riel. In 1976 he became the first Native cabinet minister in the federal government. Today he is a member of the Senate.

When I first met Len, his astonishingly clean and polished look became my conception of him. As usual, this first impression influenced how I decided to portray my subject. The composition in greys gives a clean look and the grey flannel suit suggests the white-collar image of a politician.

Senator Len Marchand

Senator Len Marchand agreed to come to my studio, and when I picked him up at his hotel that first powerful impression cemented my decision of how he must be painted. His navy overcoat, black hair, holiday tan with white teeth and white collar, made me want to do a "clean" painting. As he was a politician, it seemed appropriate to paint the man in a grey flannel suit.

We had planned to have sittings at the studio when he came to Vancouver, but it never seemed to work out, so the following summer I went to Kamloops, stayed with Len and his wife Donna and completed the painting. Once I had the opportunity to learn more about Len Marchand, my first impression was confirmed. His nature, his home and his approach to life were organized and meticulous. I set up my easel in the upstairs den and proceeded to paint "the man in the grey flannel suit".

Born in 1933 of the Okanagan tribe on the Okanagan Indian Reserve, Len Marchand came from a family of eight children. He lived on the reserve until he was twenty-three years old and graduated from the University of British Columbia in Agriculture in 1958. He worked with the Range Research Station in Kamloops and the Agricultural Research Station in Smithers as a summer student. In 1961 he went to the University of Idaho for his Master's degree; his thesis subject dealt with sagebrush in British Columbia.

From there to politics? He believes it was a matter of being the right person, in the right place, at the right time. He began by becoming involved with Indian organizations such as the North American Indian Brotherhood. People such as George Manuel and Bill Mussel felt there should be a Native person in a minister's office in some capacity, and Len was the right person.

At that time Prime Minister Lester B. Pearson was forming the new Department of Indian Affairs and Northern Development for a greater concentration on the problems of Native people. Len joined the staff and in 1968, ran against Davie Fulton as an MP and to his surprise, won.

He was eleven years an MP, secretary to Jean Chretien when he was Minister of Indian Affairs, parliamentary secretary to Mme. Jean Sauve when she was Minister of the Environment and Fisheries; then on to Minister of Small Business, and in 1977 was appointed Minister of the Environment. In June 1984, Len Marchand was made a Senator. Quite a progression from the Okanagan Reserve to the Senate. When I asked Senator Marchand about the Liberal party, these were his comments:

"I'm really a philosophical Liberal, I believe in simple terms, the middle road; I don't like the extremes. We are the enterprise party, but with a difference; we have a social philosophy. The Liberal party brought in medicare, the old age security and unemployment insurance, the Canada Assistance Plan, and the Canada Pension Plan. These kinds of things give ordinary people, all people in all walks of life, security in their lives if they are unemployed, or they become old or ill. I feel very comfortable with this kind of philosophy. . . . After all, the most important resource in our nation is people.

"This contrasts the Conservatives which is a free enterprise party and tends to favor big business. There are all kinds of examples of how that works. They have never had a social policy that compares to ours in the Liberal party.

"On the other hand, you get the other extreme, you get the NDP which is socialist. The main area where they differ from us is in their economic policy, and in the course of their economic policy they like to socialize real things. They like to see the state involved in too many parts of people's lives, especially in economic matters. I don't like that. I like to see individuals be able to do what they want, and be able to express themselves to the maximum of their ability in whatever they do."

Len also had thoughts on Riel and the Conservative government:

"These are pieces of history we are relaying. It was a Conservative government that reacted against Louis Riel and this is one of the reasons the people of Quebec say that they have never elected a Conservative leader in their party, and why the Conservatives have never done very well in the province of Quebec.

"Louis Riel was half-French and half-Indian, and they didn't have the sense and the understanding to realize that what Riel was really trying to do was to protect the rights of his people and make sure they had a place in this nation, rather than get run over by a bunch of newcomers, the railroad, and so on.

"He wanted to make sure that the rights of these people had some place and that they could express themselves in this country. That was his motivation but that could not be understood by the Conservative party of that day, so they felt that the best way to deal with a guy like Riel was to bring in the troops, rather than try to understand what he was trying to express on behalf of his people."

My first impression of Senator Len Marchand still stands!

It is interesting to note that the following article from the February 20, 1989 issue of *Kahtou;* a letter from Senator Marchand, expresses Gloria George's concerns.

FIVE HUNDRED YEAR OLD MISNOMER

I noted with great interest in the December issue of *Kahtou* that you have come to loath the use of the word Indian. I agree with you, and urge you to get a good national movement going to finally correct a five hundred year old error.

The real Indians are those good citizens from India. I wonder what would have happened if Christopher Columbus was looking for China instead of India in 1492. Would we now be called Chinese?

The use of the word Inuit is finally taking hold. I really would like to see our people agree upon a word that would represent truly who we are. In the Okanagan tongue the word is *Skilwh* which would be a little difficult to use nationally. As a member of the Okanagan Nation, I for one would be willing to go along with some appropriate word like *dene*. It is meaningful and easy to say. Keep up the good work.

Senator Len Marchand
Ottawa, Ontario K1A 0A4
(Editor's note: Thank you for your comments Senator Marchand. We respect the right of each First Nation to be called by their own name. Kahtou would like to hear suggestions from our readers in an appropriate generic name to be used when speaking collectively of all First Peoples in North America.)

A tribute to a unique moment in history

Painting #26
Size: 22 x 36 (55.88 cm x 91.44 cm)
Title: A tribute to a unique moment in history

Chief James Gosnell (1924 - 1988)
Chief Joe Mathias (1943 -)
Bill Wilson (1944 -)

Native Rights Advocates

These three Native leaders are from British Columbia. The late Chief James Gosnell was Nisga'a from Aiyansh. Chief Joe Mathias is Squamish from the Lower Mainland. He is Vice-Chief of the Assembly of First Nations. Bill Wilson is Kwagiutl of Comox from Cape Mudge.

In 1984, I appeared before the Provincial and Regional Forum (made up of chiefs, counsellors, politicians, and others from the various coastal tribes of British Columbia) to ask for their support of the *Chronicles of Pride* project. I also asked for the names of three men who would represent the contribution made by the Native Indians in the clarification of the aboriginal rights clause in the new Canadian Constitution. This was the first time that Native people had, through invitation, appeared on the floor of the House of Commons. To me it was a moment in history that had to be chronicled.

The painting shows the rooftops of the Houses of Parliament in Ottawa, a swiftly moving sky, and the heads of three of the most articulate, forceful, and expressive speakers for the Native Indian nations.

James Gosnell died July 30, 1988.

Chief Joe Mathias, Bill Wilson,
James Gosnell, Chief of the Nisga'a

I had waited three and a half years to paint the great warrior, Chief James Gosnell. I had gone before the Provincial and Regional Forum, under the chairmanship of George Watts, to ask for their approval of my project. I told them I wanted to record that historic moment when the Native people of Canada were invited onto the floor of the House of Commons for the first time.

I asked for the names of three men who would signify the body of people who travelled to Ottawa to help clarify the "aboriginal rights" clause of the new Canadian Constitution. The names given to me were Chief James Gosnell, Chief Joe Mathias and Bill Wilson; all eloquent speakers and powerful politicians. They were all willing to sit for me, I think, and had been given the word, but it was up to me to catch them when I could.

At the Forum confronting this unknown force, I had known trepidation; now Gosnell was finally coming to my studio. I picked him up at the airport and to my relief drove to the studio without incident.

The first thing he said to me was, "You're going to ask me if I believe in God—well my people believed in God before your people were ever around. We were here when the Great Flood came. I believe in God: He is the centre of my being."

The fierce looking man whom I had held in my mind for three years was astoundingly here in my studio. This powerhouse of a man, whose sudden growl would have turned the blood in my veins to water, was sitting on my dais laughing. This warrior who fights for his land, who would fight and die for his people, sat before me relaxed and peaceful. Try as I might, I could not make him look fierce.

Chief James Gosnell commented on the Constitutional questions; "I want my grandchildren to be able to read in history that when they patriated the Constitution and our rights were being discussed, that we were there representing our people to make the fight on behalf of title."

Gosnell showed great optimism for the relationship of White and Native cultures. He told me that his people had given Archbishop Ted Scott, then Primate of the Anglican Church of Canada, the tribal name for Big Rock at the Mouth of the River Nass, through love and respect for this man and the position he held.

Gosnell's relationship with Tom Berger and the *Berger Report* has also given him hope for the future: "This is the first time I've seen a change in the attitude of White men toward my people, and I feel this is what is needed to allow all of us to live in harmony."

For me, James Gosnell holds a very special place in my heart. I realized, as he sat there telling me he played saxophone in the band at Aiyansh, that he was prepared to battle all his life for his people. He sounded like a loving father—one who might scoff at being called that, but nevertheless a protector of his family, their rights and their safety.

In July, 1988, he called me into the hospital, asking me to bring the painting so that he could see it once more. When he died in the first week of August, 1988, I'm sure the earth lost a beat and all nature mourned.

Chief Joe Mathias spoke with me while I painted him in the studio and at great length talked about the concept of self-government and the philosophy behind the land claims made by Aboriginals Indigenous to Canada. In a lighter vein we discussed names and how they had come about. Apparently, long ago when the government of Canada was "registering Indians", if the agent could not understand or pronounce the name given him for listing, he wrote in any English name which came to mind, and henceforth that person was known by that name. Thus, the many Anglo-Saxon names among Aboriginal people.

In August 1984, when I called Joe Mathias for the first time, he didn't show. I waited a couple of months, then called again. He said he really wasn't interested in having the portrait done. I told him it was indeed a pain in the neck, but that it should be done for history. He came—that's all I needed. He was very cooperative, seemed to enjoy it immensely and said he would now encourage Bill Wilson and James Gosnell.

He told me that it was Jean Chretien who introduced Aboriginal rights into the Constitution. He spoke to me at length about the Constitution and the responsibility of clarifying "Aboriginal rights" and injecting them into the Constitution so that they may forever be right for the people and unchangeable by any government. Chief Joe Mathias, a Squamish, had two years of University education and two years of law. He doesn't want to be a lawyer, but wants to understand the law to further his knowledge as a politician for the Aboriginals Indigenous to Canada.

The third face on the "Constitution" painting was to be Bill Wilson of Comox, Coordinator of the Musgamagw Tribal Council. The space was empty for a long time. After many telephone calls and changed appointments, the scene was set, the time arrived and finally this would be the completion of the painting, "A Tribute to a Unique Moment in History".

On February 14, 1986, Bill Wilson sat for his portrait. He told me he had graduated from the Law Faculty of the University of British Columbia fifteen years after Judge Alfred Scow and was the second Native person to go through the faculty. He was not called to the bar but has worked in Native concerns ever since. There was little time for talk as Bill made many telephone calls every free moment. The sitting was calm with little discussion and within two hours every brush stroke had fallen into place and a statement had been made.

In a speech to a symposium on Aboriginal Title held in Victoria in 1983, Bill Wilson said, "The only concept of title that really means anything to me . . . and to other Native Indian people across the country is the feeling inside ourselves about our relationship with the land . . . "

"A Tribute to a Unique Moment in History" proved to be somewhat prophetic for each man in turn held the chairmanship of the First Nations Native Congress. Bill Wilson was elected chairman in 1990.

I painted her head and her heart . . .

Painting #27
Size: 14 x 24 (35.56 cm x 60.96 cm)

Brenda Taylor (1938 -)

Home/School Worker
Promoter of Native Indian Education

Brenda Taylor is Kwagiutl from Bella Bella, British Columbia. She is a Native Home/School Worker for the Vancouver School Board. She has been a counsellor for the Boarding Home Program of Bella Bella and the Boarding Home Program Indian Education Resources Centre. She initiated the Native Indian Youth Advisory Society and was a founder of the Native Youth Program of the University of British Columbia's Museum of Anthropology. She has raised funds and developed many programs to further Native Indian education.

Brenda has boundless energy for her favorite cause: the education of Native Indians. When the wheels start turning, she produces endless ideas that provide others with a sense of direction. Brenda's mind is as big as her heart, so I painted just that: her head and her heart. Any more of her would have overshadowed the statement. I used a value painting, almost monochromatic, to express my feelings.

Brenda Taylor

Brenda Taylor had been a great help to me right from the beginning. Once the initial idea and framework are established in a project like this, there is often someone ready to offer their ideas, and Brenda's name was given to me within the first half dozen contacts I made. She saw photographs of the first three paintings (Odjig, Wilson and Dunlop), and her mind started working overtime. Brenda was the first person I met during the project who had endless energy, ideas, contacts and dedication to the cause. When I painted Brenda, for she had to be included as a contributor to society in her role as Home/School Worker for the Vancouver School Board, all that I wanted to say about her was contained in the crispness and intensity of value in the paint, and in her eyes.

In September 1984, I had two sittings with Brenda, using a canvas 14 x 24. Brenda is dynamic, fun loving and lighthearted. When she talks about her job and school she goes a mile a minute. She is bright, crisp and deadly serious in her purpose.

It was through Brenda that I became involved with the Native Indian Youth Advisory Committee, who advised me to start the book and gave me the names of publishers to contact. Through that contact, I met Francis Eger, who was to work diligently with me from the fall of 1984 until early 1988. Francis pushed me into touring British Columbia with *Chronicles of Pride* and lecturing throughout the province.

The book was not ready, would not be ready until five years later. The project rolled along and always Brenda was there to suggest something, introduce me to someone, think of another way, because she believed in *Chronicles of Pride*, and when she believes in something, she is completely committed.

Brenda has raised millions of dollars for Native education projects from provincial and federal grants as well as private contributions. She has focused attention on the needs of Native students and without her dedication many programs now offered would not be available. She spearheaded multicultural and Native Indian education conferences such as "Educators' Conference: Multiculturalism", "Multiculturalism in Canada", and the 1987 "World Conference, Indigenous Education", along with others. To quote Brenda: "It is through these forums and the follow-up activities that change toward equality and opportunity will result."

The title Home/School Worker for the Vancouver School Board does not really do justice to Brenda Taylor's abilities and contributions to the Native cause. She has been the instigator of societies, programs, job creation, educational conferences and still works tirelessly for what she believes in. She helps, cajoles and charges on to new visions; and besides that, she is a great-grandmother! She is known and respected by many, and if she ever retires, who will be the recipient of her "little black book", which contains contacts and information that lead to miraculous developments in education?

. . . mother to twenty-three children, and grandmother to forty-five.

Painting #28
Size: 20 x 24 (50.8 cm x 60.96 cm)

Mildred Gottfriedson (1918 - 1989)

Canadian Mother of the Year, 1964

Mildred Gottfriedson was a Shuswap from the Kamloops Reserve in Kamloops, British Columbia. She was awarded Kamloops Good Citizen of the Year in 1963; British Columbia Mother of the Year in 1963 and Canadian Mother of the Year in 1964. She raised twenty-three children and has forty-five grandchildren. In 1967 she was awarded the City of Kamloops Outstanding Citizen, and on July 11, 1977, Mildred was awarded the Order of Canada and was the first Native Indian in Canada to receive such an honor.

Mildred did much in the political field to help the Native Indian people, including rallying for voting rights for women within their bands and federal voting rights for all Native people. In later life, with the same energy and determination, she began a new career as a fashion designer.

I wanted to paint Mildred as if she were on a medal. It was my tribute to her.

Mildred died in November, 1989.

Mildred Gottfriedson

While in Kamloops I was led to Mildred Gottfriedson. Millie had been the British Columbia and Canadian Mother of the Year in 1964, having raised twenty-three children and in turn, being grandmother to a mere forty-five. The concept for the painting was based on that. Only the head and shoulders of this kind-faced woman was necessary—as if placed on a medal.

On September 17, 1984, she saved time out of her busy schedule for me while she was in Vancouver to practise and take part in the ceremonies during the visit of Pope John Paul II at BC Place.

On October 9, 1984, she arrived at my studio for the second sitting at six in the morning in the pitch dark, and I put her on the noon bus back to Kamloops. With a belief in God's guidance, she was returning to Kamloops to start a new career: a business in women's dress design, something she had always wanted to do.

Senator Len Marchand told me of Mildred and felt she should be a part of my series. She was born in Kamloops of the Shuswap Nation. Most of her siblings were wiped out by the great influenza epidemic, along with thousands of her people. With almost no education, Mildred Gottfriedson has accomplished what few women do with a university degree.

Mildred Gottfriedson interview:

"In my younger days, I was taught by my father to be a good horseback rider, learn about horses, everything about stock. When I was a little older my father started teaching me how to ride and be a jockey. During those days, women were not really allowed to be jockeys, but I guess I really got away with it because I was an Indian. I used to jockey a bit for a lot of racehorse men because I was really tiny. I don't think I weighed any more than 110 pounds and I wasn't afraid of horses. It came naturally to me. I think it is one of the highlights of my young life; I really liked jockeying.

"I was about seventeen when I first met my husband. We had Kamloops Stampede Days and my husband was a bronc rider, and I was a jockey. My husband worked for a big ranching firm in Kamloops. Before we had any children I used to cowboy with him.

"There were three of us women from the interior that were selected to be trained by Andrew Paull in some of the political issues that he was involved with. My husband and I both got involved. Then we started looking at the education system. In order for our children to go beyond grade eight and to go to university, we had to look at provincial schools.

"For quite a number of years we fought the way the education system was set up. We negotiated with Indian Affairs to have Native tuition fees paid because we said that we were not going to have our children go through the same thing that we did. We had to fight very hard to get our children into provincial schools. We started talking about changes in some parts of the Indian Act.

"The first thing we succeeded in was allowing the women to vote at the band level. We had to present a Resolution from pretty well all the bands in the interior to change that part[Section 12(1)(B)] of the Indian Act. We had to present our Resolution to the Federal government, to the Department of Indian Affairs. From there we got the women the right to vote on the band level, the right to speak at band meetings.

"Then we started working on the provincial and federal vote. . . . all this in 1957. It was 1960 before we finally got the provincial and federal vote for the Indian people in the province of British Columbia. So we started looking at the women who have lost their status and why they've lost it. We've always questioned ourselves, why did Section 12(1)(B) come into the Indian Act? Why? We've questioned some of the elders, we've questioned some of the old people before they passed on. Why? Why was that section put there? It's a hard question to answer.

"We did a lot of research; where did it come from? We have found there was no consultation with the Indian people. The Indian Act was introduced to the Indian people and to the government. We never found out where it came from. The only thing we could think of was that by having Section 12(1)(B) in the Indian Act, gradually the Indian Nation would be dissolved. They knew the beliefs of our Indian people—we must not marry our cousins—and women would have to leave the reserve. Pretty soon there would be no Indians left. That's the only answer that we could come up with.

"Now, maybe I'm wrong, but we've done a lot of research on this and we can't seem to come up with an answer. In some cases they don't even allow the women to go back on the reserve to visit. It's not just the government. It's the attitude that has developed. We hear this all the time; a lot of the Indian people blame the government, but it is up to the Indian people to change some of the things that are happening. If we could only unify in

B.C. and fight for what is right. I think the Indian people are their own worst enemy. That is really true. Indian people have to come together and join hands and fight for the rights of their people. The Indian people are hurting themselves because of their philosophy.

"I think what I'm trying to say is that we have a lot of fight ahead of us with our own people. In 1970, we presented our policy paper to the Department of Indian Affairs. Who was the minister of Indian Affairs? It was Jean Chretien. He was very sympathetic with us at that time. We pointed out we wanted section Section 12(1)(B)deleted from the Indian Act.

"If total self-government is given to the Indian people and they want to do away with the Department of Indian Affairs, where are they going to negotiate? They won't have a place to go. I sure wouldn't want to see our own people govern us because there is too much discrimination among our leaders . . . How are they going to do it? I believe in self-government within your *own* band. Advanced bands look after the education system, they look after housing, they look after every other business that they have to administer. If they want Indian self-government they would have to follow the traditions of our people; that is kindness and honesty. If the band is fortunate enough to have a development of their own, the revenues that they have from their band still have to go to the Treasury Board.

"In 1980, the B.C. Native Women's Society made their first presentation to the House of Commons with their policy paper. In 1981, the B.C. Native Women's Society presented their policy paper at the world conference in Geneva—at the World's Human Rights Commission. We were heard and they definitely stated that Section 12(1)(B) of the Indian Act was discriminatory. So from then on, we really had the government listening to the women."

In the fight against Section 12(1)(B) of the Indian Act, Mildred was instrumental in the presentation of Bill C-31 which gives status back to the non-status Native women. Mildred Gottfriedson was not only a mother to so many children, both Indian and non-Indian, but she has been a caring mother to her people.

. . . a man of great vision, insight and compassion.

Painting # 29
Size: 24 x 34 (60.96 cm x 86.36 cm)
Title: Tribute to Robert Sterling

Robert Sterling (1937-1983)

Educator

Robert (Thumper) Sterling was of the Thompson Indian Nation, Lower Nicola Valley Band at Merritt, British Columbia. He was an educator of outstanding ability and instigated the Native Indian Home/School Coordinator Program in British Columbia. He was also instrumental in developing the Native Indian Teacher Education Program at the University of British Columbia. He headed the Nicola Valley Indian Education Administration in Merritt until his death.

Robert accepted my invitation to be a part of this series. Shortly afterward he died, along with his son, in an accident on the Thompson River. After great deliberation, and not having met Robert, I decided I could not do a portrait. I would have to do a study showing many faces and pray that I would do this well-loved man justice. The composition of the picture was worked out on the back of an envelope, late one night at the kitchen table. It was a composite of faces I had seen on videos I borrowed from the Ministry of Education and the University of British Columbia.

Robert Sterling

Robert Sterling: educator—a man of great vision, insight and compassion. I had written to him early in 1982 to ask him to be part of my project, and he had responded with humility: "I would be proud to be a part of such a project."

When I was advised of the drowning accident which claimed the life of Robert Sterling and of his son, I was determined to include him in the series at all costs. I delayed painting him until I could freely turn my mind to the idea of a man who seemed to be so close to the hearts of so many people.

I went to Merritt, British Columbia, to speak with his successor, Mandy Jimmy, the people he had worked with, and his family. I had to rely on my instincts and listen carefully to whatever messages went through my head. Robert's mother had given me his graduation picture and one snap of him; hardly enough to paint a portrait. I had seen a videotape in Merritt, had made sketches and had become aware of the planes and contours of Robert's face.

When I returned to Vancouver I contacted the university and the Ministry of Education and found videotapes of his last speech. I heard his message, saw his body language, and made my decisions. The canvas was stretched, sketches were made and I developed a composition on the back of an envelope at the kitchen table late one night.

Never so clearly have I received help from some hidden source while under the influence of oil and turpentine. Usually, contact with your creative nature or the subjective part of your mind is through your diaphragm. The chord seems to travel from that area up through your body, your mind and out your arm to the end of your fingers, to the end of your paintbrush and to the point of contact with the canvas.

However, inspiration and direction came through what seemed to be a tiny hole in the side of my right temple, and by the time I had finished the painting, I felt I had been directed well and it all hung together. I was still concerned as to the likeness I had captured or the statement I had made about a man I had never met. The next day Mandy Jimmy and Lorraine Moses came to the studio with the verification.

After much thought I chose to do five heads of him in an arc with the abstract mouth of a whale behind him—to me the whale mouth depicted "a whale of a speaker". The heads were all mobile with different attitudes, though all heads showed warmth, amusement, sincerity and caring.

At one point when I added a cold color to the background, I heard the word through the small hole in my right temple—"sacrilegious". I quickly painted on a warmer color and felt much better about it.

As I looked at the painting I became concerned that it was not a portrait per se. I then heard the word "tribute", and again rested easy. When I put the last brush stroke on the canvas, I felt I must have someone who had known him see it, to assure me that I had produced a painting which made the statement I intended. Again I heard the message: call Mandy Jimmy in Merritt. I called and she was coming to Vancouver the next day.

Lorraine said she had "never seen him [Robert] with a scowl on his face, always he was kind. He had an impish look often. When most people spoke they became very serious; he always retained a pleasant look that could break into a smile." From Mandy: "There was nothing that could offend or give the wrong feeling about the man."

"Success in Indian Education: A Sharing" was a conference conducted by NITEP in 1984 with the proceeds from the accompanying publication to be donated to the Robert W. Sterling Memorial NITEP Award. The following are some notes from that publication:

Dedication

These proceedings are meant to serve as a testimony to the great spirit of the conference entitled "Successes in Indian Education: A Sharing", which took place February 17, 18 and 19, 1983 in Vancouver, British Columbia.

One of the deep inspirational sources for this memorable event was **Robert W. Sterling,** an invincible spirit, a universal man, who dedicated the greatest part of his life to the improvement of Indian Education. To many of his friends and colleagues, the conference exemplified Robert's life-long devotion, faith and dream.

These proceedings are dedicated to the memory and works of **Robert W. Sterling,** remembered by so many as an exceptional and wonderful man. May his works, words and philosophy, of kindness, sharing and dedication, guide us in gaining a better understanding of ourselves and others, and in reaching fulfillment as human beings.

Robert and his oldest child Corey, passed away in a tragic canoe accident on the Thompson River near Spences Bridge, a few days after the closing of the conference.

(biographical notes reproduced with permission of Doreen Sterling)

. . . many young people came to visit and ask advice of this wise, beautiful, elderly woman.

Painting #30
Size: 24 x 30 (60.96 cm x 76.2 cm)

Agnes Alfred (1889(?) -)

Elder

Agnes Alfred, a Kwagiutl elder, was born on Village Island near Alert Bay, British Columbia. Since the history of Native culture is oral, it is the responsibility of elders, like Agnes Alfred, to hold it close and pass on all songs, dances, family places, and happenings that form the history of Native culture.

In 1922, Agnes Alfred was jailed for participating in an outlawed potlatch held in the area of her homeland. She later participated in the re-enactment of this forbidden ceremony when it was filmed by the National Film Board in "Potlatch: A Strict Law Bids Us Dance". Many artifacts were confiscated from various tribes at the potlatch of 1922 and sold to collectors as far away as New York.

This is a primatura ("one sitting") painting. Two hours into the painting, I was advised I had only another two hours to finish it. Agnes sat weaving a basket while many young people visited her, seeking the advice and guidance of this wise, wonderful, elderly woman.

Agnes Alfred

When you are involved with so many people, such as the 37 people involved in *Chronicles of Pride*, it seems reasonable that you might encounter some specific hardships along the way. The painting of Agnes Alfred proved no exception to the rule. On the contrary, everything went wrong, and unfortunately, I never consider putting something off until everything is easy.

The airlines lost my paints and easel, although they turned up later on, so I had to find supplies in Campbell River; although I had made arrangements by telephone, on arrival I could not contact Agnes. When I finally found her and was two hours into the painting I discovered I had only a total of four hours in which to capture her because the family was leaving for a meeting.

Although I went to very great lengths to ensure my sound equipment was working and accurate, on my return home I wearily listened while no sound issued forth from the speakers. Agnes had told me stories of her youth, had sung songs for me in her own language, while her grand-daughter Dora Cook interpreted the words—an extraordinary tape; and I missed it. I knew I must be coming to the end of my work.

During the painting, Agnes wove a basket and spoke with many young people who came to visit and ask advice of this wise old lady. In the interview we laughed together when Agnes couldn't quite remember if she was ninety-two or ninety-six, but we agreed the years meant nothing. It's what she is and has been that's important. Her birth is recorded on a rock on Village Island, British Columbia, and if anyone needs to know they can find out.

The people in this project had been good enough to give me their time so it is fortunate that I am able to capture the likeness and spirit of a person as quickly as I do. It comes from years of concerted effort in the field of portraiture. In the years needed to learn my skill, the repetition of form and character over and over again prepared me for this project. It allowed me to paint, and yet to put all my concentration into understanding and expressing the nature of the subject. The technique of using thin washes of turpentine and oil, and building up to an impasto allows that moment of truth when, with paintbrush and paint, one breathes life into a painting and celebrates the positive life forces.

Agnes Alfred had been part of that ceremony often mistakenly called the "last potlatch", in 1922. It was not the last potlatch, but it stood out because many of the participants were imprisoned—the government had decided to make their move. Agnes was one of those imprisoned for her participation in the ritual which had been outlawed by the government.

Now, at this great age, she holds the unique position of being one of the few remaining elders of a Native culture. The elder, most important for the balance of my series, and certainly for his or her culture, is given great respect because it is he or she who passes on to the younger ones the history, the culture and the rules to live by. What Agnes says is never taken lightly. She has seen many changes, many injustices in her lifetime and still she remains uncomplaining, ready to offer assistance and guidance whenever she is needed.

Agnes Alfred, along with the other subjects of *Chronicles of Pride,* are much needed role models and should be used as guidelines for our own lives. And we should always be aware of the strength of character in *all* cultures and races.

I was overwhelmed by the feeling of promise.

Painting #31
Size: 48 x 48 (121.92 cm x 121.92 cm)
Title: A Promise

Native Youth Group: A Promise
Vernon Mulvahill, Don Bain, Lori Speck,
Eileen Joe and Sadie Morris

On the completion of the painting of Agnes Alfred, I thought that *Chronicles of Pride* was ended. However, one year later I met five young Native people rediscovering their culture through the Native Youth Program at the University of British Columbia's Museum of Anthropology. I was overwhelmed by the feeling of promise. Vernon Mulvahill, Don Bain, Lori Speck, Eileen Joe, and Sadie Morris are a sample of the future. Each one has a remarkable depth of character and faith. Within them grows a promise that the Native Indian people will survive as a culture.

These young people embody hope and in my mind their portraits form the best conclusion for *Chronicles of Pride*.

A Promise

On completion of the painting of Agnes Alfred in March of 1985, I felt *Chronicles of Pride* was ended. I didn't realize that the series was not complete. We tried to start the book too soon.

There was a unanimous feeling that the biographies of my subjects should be written by a Native person to give validity to the book. Different writers were approached but not until Val Dudoward appeared on the scene did any work get done. Val produced and worked very hard, but that was not the way it was to be.

The frustrations that I had gone through trying to get the book completed and published suddenly became an overwhelming burden in August 1987. After four full years of constant work toward that end, I at last felt beaten to the point of walking away from it all. I prayed to the Creator asking for guidance, and of course, the answer came.

I had been asked by Gloria George to speak to the Native Youth Group at the UBC Museum of Anthropology. Gloria wanted me to show the young people the slide presentation of *Chronicles of Pride* and tell them how it had all come about, and of the contributions to society of those I had painted. They were a small group, five in number, and although I only spent the morning with them I strongly felt a newness and a promise in them.

I awoke the next morning with the completed painting before my eyes and knew that here was the answer I had cried out for. Here was the completion to the series, the conclusion, a promise of a new world.

I called the same morning and made the arrangements. The young people were delighted to stand among the ancient poles while I painted a 4 x 4 foot canvas showing the presence, the vision, the love that I had seen in this group who were the "natural resource" of a people in transition. They are a sample of the future, filled with a remarkable depth of character and faith. Within them grows a promise that Native Indians, the Aboriginal people of our land, will survive. The five students were Vernon Mulvahill, Don Bain, Lori Speck, Eileen Joe and Sadie Morris.

Conclusion

Although I had wanted to paint George Clutesi and many others, I realized my work was done, my statement made. The next step was to make sure the exhibit was seen by as many people as possible. A first showing was arranged for April 15, 1986 at the Museum of Anthropology, University of British Columbia.

With thanks to Pacific Western Airlines and Canadian Pacific Airlines (now combined as Canadian Airlines International), a British Columbia tour was arranged for the year 1987. Although they were the carriers for the nine exhibitions, thirteen northern cities actually hung the exhibitions and many adults and hundreds of children attended the showings. Some were bussed from outlying districts as far as eighty miles away, some would walk ten to twenty blocks in the snow. Some classes came who were all Métis, some were senior art students, even a broadcasting class. They all wanted to know, to learn, to hear about the people I had painted, contemporary Canadian Native Indians and their accomplishments.

Excerpts from my notes on the *Chronicles of Pride* tour through British Columbia:

"Due to Fran Eger's generosity of spirit my service as a speaker was offered and duly noted because in all of the tour so far, school children have come, usually seventy-five to one hundred a day.

"My rewards for this long effort, if rewards there must be, have been the guileless remarks and actions of the children. A Dene youth from the Northwest Territories who was at the show with a group from a broadcasting school was overwhelmed by the colors in the paint and the fact that someone actually painted people. He'd never seen anything like it before, and then to hear the contributions that these people had made—his eyes were wide in amazement, a new awareness growing. Another young fellow spent at least two hours looking at the work and afterwards came over and discussed the colors I'd used and what the people had done, and then said, 'they must love you for what you've done'."

A tall girl dressed in a jean jacket covered in rhinestones, towered above me, pumped my hand and thanked me. As I was speaking to a group of elementary students, I found myself standing behind a young boy with my hands lightly on his upper arms near his shoulders. Without stopping the talk, I looked around him to see that it was a young Native boy. As the class moved on, I naturally thought the boy would move on also. He never moved a muscle. His attention was riveted on the paintings. Later, he came to speak to me, found a small scrap of paper and asked for my autograph.

The teacher and teaching assistant had seen the incident and were very moved by it. They explained that this boy was a problem in the classroom, and it was quite unusual to see him so focused and involved.

I found Native students made a point of standing immediately beside the painting of the person I was speaking about, trying to relate. I made a point of visiting Friendship Centres in all the communities and of making myself known to the Director and inviting them to the exhibit. At one exhibit there was an alternative school, mostly of Native students who had not fit in to the regular school system. I wondered how these students would be. They were polite, attentive and asked good questions. One girl in her teens stood about a foot away from the paintings, looking alternately at them and listening intently. Finally, on her way out she said, "Can we write to you?"

The classes went from Grades 1 to 12. I received letters from the children, hugs from the teachers, and invitations to go to their schools, Moberly Lake school being one.

In this long and arduous endeavor I have found that the project has taken on a life of its own. I do not control it. No individual has control over it. We work together toward an end, and every day is a surprise.

If some stories are longer than others, it doesn't make anyone less or more important, but possibly it means some people were more vocal than others, or that I was particularly interested in the message being conveyed to the readers of this book so they too could begin to have a new understanding.

Although the original concept of the chapters was to be biographical notes on the subjects painted, it has evolved into a story of warm relationships and a sense of wonder of the energy expended by people who, in their everyday lives, try so hard to do the best they can possibly do and in so doing make a significant contribution to life. I leave biographical statistical writings to those who do them well.

With the thirty-one paintings that make up the series *Chronicles of Pride,* I have tried to convey that love, spirituality and wealth of human resources within a culture.

It is a natural phenomenon that we turn away from things that we know nothing about. It is easier in the struggle of life to just stick close and develop our understanding of things within our own environment. As growth is necessary for all things, it is also necessary for attitude.

The most important attribute I wished to convey in the paintings is their human dignity. We are told that all men, women and children should give and receive "the respect due his fellow man, woman or child". If, through my work I can make some minor contribution to an attitude of living, then I believe I have been a successful artist. The book will carry my success beyond the gallery wall.

Acknowledgments

To the Minister of State, Multiculturalism and Citizenship, and the recent Minister of Indian Affairs, David Crombie who have supported me in this program I give my thanks.

The late Francis H. Eger was a driving force that pushed me in so many ways, always convinced of my ability, encouraging me to do things I would never have dreamed of doing, introducing me to areas I had never known. Without her dynamic presence in the project it would have taken far more than the seven years that is now banked up on one side of the ledger.

Valerie Dudoward worked diligently in the first writing of *Chronicles of Pride* but as we have found, the project took on a life of its own and continued along another route. Charles Lillard found the concept exciting and suggested using the dialogue from those tapes that I did at the time of the sittings. Lila Kilroy appeared on the scene and quietly dogged my footsteps until the book was written. My never tiring typist—"one that excels the quirks of blazoning pens"—Judith Filtness was there to correct my mistakes, to patiently type and retype page after page.

My husband withstood the difficulties of living with a workaholic with amazing grace. My family and friends showed great patience at my tenacity and encouraged me in my endeavor over a long seven year period. And Georges Erasmus, National Chief Assembly of First Nations who graciously commented on the content.

To the many, many people who have been involved in the networking and production of the project *Chronicles of Pride*, I give my gratitude. They cannot all be named, there are so many, but they know that they have been a part of something much bigger than all of us.

Air BC, Pacific Western and Canadian Airlines International have assisted beyond measure. And to those fine people who formed the subject matter of this tale, I give my thanks, for without them the story could not have been told. I only pray that the telling will be one large step toward the understanding and communication of all people.

All Glory to the Creator whose power,
working in us,
can do infinitely more than we can ask or imagine.

JPL